Domestic Violence and Abuse

How to stop it !

CALIFORNIA EDITION

By Cheryl Anne Woodard
California Attorney, Certified
Family Law Specialist

Edited by Ed Sherman
California Attorney

NOLO PRESS OCCIDENTAL

PO Box 722 • Occidental, CA 95465 • (707) 874-3105

What's your story?

The author is interested in your experience in stopping domestic violence in your life. If you would like to share your story, or give us your feedback or comments about this book, please write to the author at 12304 Santa Monica Boulevard, Suite 300, Los Angeles, CA 90025. Sorry, but she can't promise to answer all letters. No phone calls, please.

DATED MATERIAL
THIS BOOK WAS PRINTED IN
JANUARY, 1996

DO NOT USE AN OLD PRINTING OF THIS BOOK!
OUT OF DATE = DANGEROUS

Laws and forms change fairly often, usually in January and July. That's why this book is printed at least twice each year, to give you the latest information. Using an old printing of this book can be dangerous if the information or forms in it are wrong! **Make sure you are using the most current printing.** If the date above is over one year old, you are taking chances.

FIRST EDITION

First Printing	January 1996
Editor	ED SHERMAN
Typography	STEPHEN POLLARD
Research	LORIE LEIGH ROBERTSON
Printing	DIVERSIFIED PRINTING, BREA, CALIFORNIA
Acct. Executive	RANDY HOLUBICZKO
Forms	MARTIN DEAN'S ESSENTIAL FORMS

Although great care has been taken to ensure the accuracy and utility of the information and forms contained in this book, no warranty is made, express or implied, and neither Nolo Press nor the authors assume any liability in connection with any use or result from use of the information or forms contained herein.

© 1996 by Cheryl Anne Woodard

ISBN 0-944508-23-5
Library of Congress No. 95-71147

TABLE OF CONTENTS

PART TWO: HOW TO STOP DOMESTIC ABUSE

Battered women's shelters and temporary emergency housing
How to find a shelter near you
Domestic violence counseling
Support groups
Legal advice and domestic violence law clinics
Other groups: 12-step and substance abuse
Growing pains

How to use informal support
Who can you use for informal support?
Checklist for your support network

Tell him to stop! Exactly what to say
Expose him
Protect your space
Ask for what you want or need
Be alert. Avoid what sets him off
Build your case
Get a restraining order
How to get the police on your side
Things to avoid
    Do not expect to change him
    Do not go to counseling with him
Things to do
    Ask for a court-approved program for batterers
    Study books on domestic violence
Going underground—not recommended

Elisa
Delia
Helen
Martha

PART THREE: PREPARING FOR LEGAL ACTION

7. Bank Accounts
   Right to funds
   Taking funds for support
8. Cars
9. Businesses
10. Guns
11. Lost earnings and expenses
12. Immigration issues
13. Interpreters
14. Attorney fees and court costs.

PART FOUR: HOW TO GET YOUR RESTRAINING ORDER

Foreword

Are you in a safe place right now?

This book is about how to stop domestic abuse that ranges from irritating harassment to full-blown violence.

If you are living with a violent person or one who may become violent, do not read this book or work on the forms where he can catch you at it. Use this book at work in your free time, or at a library, courthouse, or some other quiet place. Do not store this book or the papers you are working on at home. Keep them at a friend's house or in a secure place at work.

Consider whether it is safe for you to stay any longer with this person. If at any point you feel you are in danger, go to a shelter or other safe place and work on this from there.

Reasoning with him

If your mate is a chronic batterer, experience tells us that reasoning with him and trying to help him change is a losing proposition. It is draining, probably futile and possibly dangerous. If you already know he is intractable, do not attempt to reason with him. It is time now to focus on what you can do to help yourself.

Do not attempt to discuss this book with him, and do not waste time trying to figure him out or trying to help him change. Concentrate on your situation and what you can do to improve it.

Regaining your power

It is time to stop letting his ideas dominate your thinking. Watch your thoughts. If you find that almost everything you think is couched in his terms, his ideas, his "truth," and what he wants, then your job is to take back your own thinking and your own power.

As you progress, note your thoughts and work on developing your own ideas. You will begin to have ideas that ring true in your heart and mind. It will be your own thinking. Welcome back.

How to use this book

This book offers practical advice about how to stop domestic violence in your life. It also shows you exactly how to go to court and get a Domestic Violence Restraining Order. These orders will restrain a husband, boyfriend, household member, parent of your child, or family members from abusing you or your children or other members of your household. If you are being abused by a person in some other type of relationship—a neighbor, an employer, a stranger—you may need a type of legal action not covered in this book.

Read the Table of Contents and note passages that fit your situation. Read those first. For example, if you have been attacked by your partner, there is no need to dwell on Chapter 1 where we discuss how to recognize abuse—you *know* you are being beaten! Go directly to Part Two and get some advice about dealing with emergencies. Return later to the more general information.

Throughout this book you will be urged to seek the advice of experienced domestic abuse counselors and find help at battered women's shelters and domestic violence support groups. *Please heed this advice!* This is the single most important thing you can do for yourself. What you are going through is traumatic, personal and individual. This book can't handle every item you need and it can't replace skilled individual advice and the comfort of a human presence. *Please* take care to get your advice from a counselor who is qualified and experienced in domestic abuse; not just any counselor or lawyer can help you.

Help for a friend. If you are reading this book to find help for a friend or relative, please read Appendix A about how to be someone's support person.

Gender language. This book uses "he" for the perpetrator, since the perpetrator is male in over 90% of all abuse cases. Women can also be abusive, and abusive behaviors can be found in close family or same-sex relationships. The point here is to understand the continuum of abuse and learn what you can do to stop it.

PART ONE

RECOGNIZING THE PROBLEM

Chapter 1

Does this describe your life?

preventing

The behaviors listed below are common to abusive relationships and are listed in escalating order. It is important to understand that abuse can begin as disrespect which, if unchecked, can escalate into full-blown, lethal violence. This list can help you understand if you are in an abusive and potentially violent relationship. Check off the items that apply. The more items checked, the more potentially dangerous your situation is. The further down the list you are, the more danger you are in. Pay special attention to the signs of danger, because some men have been known to suddenly leap from low-order harassment to life-threatening violence.

Not everyone who makes a disrespectful remark is an abusive person or on the verge of violence. Look at these behaviors as a reality check. But if something feels wrong to you, it probably *is* wrong. Some of us have stopped trusting our feelings. We have been so undermined that we lose touch with our own sense of "rightness." Call it intuition, call it feelings. You will be asked here to look at this and you will be asked to start trusting yourself. At some point in your life you must learn again to trust your own feelings. Start now. If someone has you "walking on eggs," or makes your life miserable with behaviors like these, you are in an abusive relationship and it could get worse. Consider taking some action to prevent the situation from escalating and to protect yourself before it is too late for you and your children.

pay attention what is happening — thild around again trust your feelings

List of escalating abusive behaviors

This is about behavior that is repeated. A truly rare bad episode is not at all the same thing as a recurring pattern.

1. Disrespect, attacks on your self-esteem *emotional abuse*

✦ He is disrespectful in the way he speaks to you. For example, he calls you derogatory names. He criticizes the way you look and what you do in a destructive way. He acts as if you can't do anything right and you begin to believe him. You lose your self-confidence and sense of self-worth.

✦ When something goes wrong, he blames you. Everything is your fault. He is frequently suspicious and accuses you of wrongdoing.

✦ He yells at you and swears at you.

✦ He makes humiliating, embarrassing, or belittling remarks. He makes them in front of others. He ridicules you, your friends and your family.

✦ He erupts into tirades, violent fits of screaming anger.

✦ He takes his own bad behavior very lightly. What are you so upset about? He didn't abuse you, you provoked him. It's all *your* fault. He shifts responsibility away from himself and blames you.

2. Pressure, manipulation and control

After disrespect comes control. This is the next step toward more apparent forms of violence. He is pushing you around mentally and verbally.

✦ He interrupts, refuses to listen or to take seriously what you have to say.

✦ He twists what you say, and turns your words against you.

✦ He tells you what to do, and tries to make you feel bad, guilty or wrong if you do not do what he wants.

✦ He insists that his ideas are "right," and that you are wrong.

✦ What he says is the "truth"; he says that you are confused.

✦ He rushes you into making decisions.

✦ He pouts and sulks if you do not do what he wants.

✦ He uses the children against you. He teaches them to be disrespectful of you. They are conflicted and do not understand why.

✦ He shapes your life. He knows what is best for you; he acts as your teacher and guide. You believe he knows what is best and your judgment becomes replaced by his.

3. Economic control, isolation
Economic control and isolation can become imprisonment.

✦ He refuses to let you work. He undermines or interferes with your work, either subtly or overtly. He refuses to let you go to school or start a career.

✦ He is the sole support of the family and refuses to give you money. If you have any money, he takes it or controls the amount you can have.

✦ He takes your car or your car keys, or otherwise prevents you from getting around.

✦ He controls your time, who you spend time with. He tells you who you can see, where you can and can't go.

✦ He monitors phone calls and insists on knowing where you have been. You have to account for your time.

✦ He frequently checks up on you.

Some abusive partners control diplomatically, but nevertheless they control you. They arrange circumstances and finances so that you can't make a move without their approval. They do not yell or scream, but you are still controlled and imprisoned. If you feel trapped, it is probably because you *are* trapped. If this is your situation, be alert to the other behaviors listed here and the risk of escalation discussed below.

4. Harassment, repetition, hounding
Some people are obsessive or inappropriate in other ways. This can manifest itself as repetition: he repeats his statements over and over until he wears you down.

✦ He makes uninvited visits or calls.

✦ He refuses to leave when asked.

✦ He follows you.

✦ He embarrasses you in public.

5. Signals of increasing danger

The following behaviors are clear indications that the situation is escalating and the danger increasing. The behavior is becoming more physical, and if he throws something at you one day, he could throw *you* the next.

Physical menacing or intimidation

✦ He makes angry or threatening gestures.

✦ He towers over you in a menacing way.

✦ He stands in a doorway during an argument, or corners you, blocking your escape.

✦ He drives recklessly while you are in the car.

✦ He throws things, breaks things, punches the wall, kicks in a door, throws something out the window.

Threats

✦ He threatens you or your family. If he does this, you must take these threats seriously.

Pushing and shoving

✝ Pushing or shoving is the beginning of more direct physical violence. If this is tolerated, the violence will escalate. This is the phase where he is testing limits to see what he can get away with. Many men do not regard this as physical, violent abuse, but *you* know it is.

Sexual pressure, assaults

Has he forced you to have sex when you did not want to? Has he forced you to perform sexually in ways degrading to you or against your will? If you tolerate this kind of behavior, it can escalate into direct physical attack and serious physical injury.

Physical violence

When you are being hit, kicked, choked, or handled in a violent way, you are being abused. If you continue to tolerate such violence and abuse, it can escalate and become lethal.

Weapons

✦   He has weapons around the house that frighten you.

✦   He threatens to use them against you.

Self-destructive behavior or talk, suicidal talk

Does he abuse drugs or alcohol? Substance abuse is dangerous because an intoxicated person has little self-control, and there is a greater potential for violence. Has he threatened suicide? Has he sabotaged his work by not showing up, performing badly, or telling off his boss? It is also self-destructive behavior. Self-destructive behavior and self-sabotage indicate depression and hopelessness; his behavior may be the result of acute mental distress.

Drugs, alcohol, weapons, hopelessness, acute mental distress; all these are indicators that the violence could become lethal.

6. Signals of extreme danger

According to the Los Angeles Police Department, the following are indicators that an abuser is extremely dangerous and may become seriously violent or kill.

✦   He has threatened to kill himself, you, the children, or family members.

✦   He is acutely depressed.

✦   He has weapons and has used them or threatened to use them.

✦   He is obsessive about you. He idolizes you, and feels that he cannot live without you. He believes that he is entitled to you.

✦   Extreme jealousy. He believes that there is another man, and if he cannot have you, no one else can.

✦   Hopelessness. He feels if he loses you he has lost all hope for a future.

✦   Extreme rage. The most life-endangering rage is said to arise when the woman leaves and that the first two months are the most dangerous. No one really knows exactly when this "critical" phase starts or ends. We *do* know that leaving this type of person must be planned and carried out with great care.

✦ Abuse of either drugs or alcohol will increase the intensity of rage, despair or other negative emotions and will impede judgment and inhibitions.

✦ Pet abuse. Batterers who torment or mutilate pets are more likely to kill or maim family members.

If any of these factors are present, you must exercise great caution in your planning. Make sure that when you do leave, there is no access. If he cannot find you or the children, he cannot harm you. This is discussed in greater detail below.

Chapter 2

The cycle of domestic violence

If you understand the cyclical nature of domestic abuse and violence, it may help you deal with it in your own life.

Abuse and violence in a domestic setting often come in cycles. These cycles were identified and described in 1979 by Dr. Lenore E. Walker in her book *The Battered Woman*.

Phase One: The Build-Up. This is the "walking on eggs" part. This is where you know trouble is brewing and building. There is tension in the air. The tension escalates. Some women actually provoke a blow-up to end the tension.

Phase Two: The Blow-Up. This is the peak of violence. It may be a tirade, throwing things, or a physical attack, depending on where you are on the continuum of escalating violence.

Phase Three: Remorse and Contrition. He feels sorry for what he has done. He apologizes, he promises that he will never do it again. He promises to change. He may bring gifts. He can be very charming, charismatic, persuasive. He might bring you gifts and flowers. He may promise to go to counseling with you, and he may go. This is the honeymoon, the seduction. You are hopeful that he will truly change. Dr. Walker notes that the one thing all women reported of their batterers was their manipulative charm in this phase.

You fear him, you love him, and you are hopeful. You take him back. Then he begins to get restless, and the tension starts building again. These phases repeat and keep repeating until the cycle is broken.

Where is your relationship in the list of abusive behavior? Do you see a pattern? Dr. Walker defined a battered woman as one who had been through this cycle twice. In other words, the woman had taken her man back twice after abusive behavior on his part. Have you been seduced into taking him back only to have the abuse repeated? It is important that you see the "honeymoon" for what it is. It is just part of a repeating cycle. Even though he promises he will never do it again, he *will* do it again unless someone or something breaks the pattern.

Breaking the pattern

You know better than anyone why you have stayed in this relationship. You may love him or remember him as someone you loved. You may have children with him, or be economically dependent upon him. You may think you have no education, training, or prospects of your own. You may have lost your confidence and have little faith in yourself.

When you try to look honestly at the situation or do something about it, you may feel overwhelmed. It is normal to feel overwhelmed at first. It is normal to feel overwhelmed a lot. Proceed anyway. You *do* have the power to leave. It may take some time to figure this out, but you *can* do it.

Practical advice about taking advice

As you recover from your own negative thinking and doubts, and as you begin to redefine your relationship, be prepared to get advice and pressure from well-meaning but unknowing family, friends or church members. When this happens, you *will* be prepared because this book explains how to find *experienced* help. If you follow our advice, you will have advisors who are trained in domestic violence counseling and understand the issues. Use your friends, family, church and social acquaintances for moral support, emotional venting, recreation and distraction, but do *not* take advice from people who are not trained and experienced in domestic violence counseling.

Going back to him

If you have tried to leave before and have gone back to him several times, you may feel you can't get away. Yes, you can. It is normal to make several attempts. It is not a crime to go back if this is what you have to do until you have a better plan. This does not mean that you can't get away ever. It just means that more is needed. Don't be discouraged; it may take several tries to leave for good. If you stick with it, you will prevail.

Making new patterns

It is important to understand that this relationship started with behavior which you tolerated. By tolerating it again and again, you allowed the pattern to continue. If you are reading this book, you do not like this pattern and you want to change it. You can create a new pattern. The purpose of this book is to help you make your change in a practical and safe way.

Emotions and how to deal with them

If part of you died inside some time ago—the part that could feel—be prepared for something new. You will begin to feel again. This, too, can add to the feeling of being overwhelmed.

How do you deal with your own feelings? Feel them. Take the time and have the courage to feel them. Do not be afraid to feel psychic pain, sadness, grief, or any of the other emotions in the healing cycle. Name your feelings. Say "I am angry" or "I am outraged"; whatever it happens to be. Once you have felt it, and have figured out what it is you are feeling, take the next step.

In the next step you choose. Look at the many ways you can handle the situation presented. Do not just let your emotions sweep you away. For example, in the course of a physical attack by him, he chases you and your two children into the laundry room and manages to lock you and one child in. He and the other child are outside the laundry room. He is screaming at you, demanding that you agree to let him have both children. Your son, outside the door, is upset and screaming for you. What do you do? Do you shriek, cry, scream and yell back? Bang on the door? Break the window? In a fit of emotion you might do this, but if you step back and think for a minute, you might think of a better response. You might send your son to a neighbor's house to call 911. This is what one woman did to successfully resolve a similar situation.

You can choose what you will do with your feelings and you can choose how you will behave. If this approach is new to you, experiment with it. This is not as simple as it sounds, but it is possible. Work on identifying your feelings, feeling them, and then choosing what you will do to take care of business.

Types of emotional responses

In dealing with the world of feelings, let's identify several types of emotional responses you may find in yourself and your partner. The first is a healthy, proactive, emotional response. This is the most empowering. Next is the typical cycle of negative emotions, and third is unhealthy, toxic rage which must be handled quite differently from the first two.

Dealing with your own emotions and those of others is one of the biggest challenges of personal relationships. The discussion below might give you some insights into this important area of your life. It is no replacement for further study or counseling where needed.

1. Healthy emotional response

Someone yells at you. You hear it as a person yelling at you and you decide how to respond—i.e. say something in reply, leave the room, etc. You also decide how you will feel after the initial reaction. In this process you may initially feel a twinge of anger, fear, guilt, distrust, or whatever. The key is that the emotion is felt and acknowledged, an action is chosen, and you move on. There is no bitterness or resentment, hostility or striking back. The emotion is not suppressed or denied, but it does not determine your reaction.

You do not have to stay with a negative emotion; you can decide not to feel hurt even though someone is attacking you verbally or emotionally. You can decide that the person doing this is upset and acknowledge his emotions without adopting them as your own. It is even helpful to say, "I see that you are very upset and angry."

Many authors call this a proactive approach in contrast to a reactive approach. This is the strongest, most powerful approach to an emotional or verbal attack. You are in control and you have not given your power away. You choose how you will respond and it may or may not be in anger, depending on what is appropriate for the circumstances. You are cool and in charge.

This does not mean that you are numb, indifferent or insensitive. It means that you choose how you will behave, and you do not let anyone choose this for you.

2. Typical cycle of negative emotions

Next comes the typical cycle of negative emotions. Often, when a desire is thwarted, we are hurt or angry. We want to blame someone. In the instant that we do this, we give our power away. We become frustrated and at this point may have lost control; we explode or smolder with anger.

If you find yourself doing this, it is possible to stop the cycle. You can stop it at the beginning, at the point when you first feel hurt and want to blame some-one. If you decide instead to take responsibility for the result, then you keep your power.

For example, let's say you wanted to go to a movie with your partner and he said no. You could be hurt and blame him for never wanting to go anywhere, or you can make different choices. You can decide that he does not want to go, that this is all right. You are not hurt because he does not want to go, and you can go with your sister, friend, etc., or you can do something else.

The point is, you can eliminate the harmful effects of negativity by changing your mind. You step out of the cycle and save yourself the grief. More impor-tant, you keep your power. There are several helpful books in this area: *Conscious Loving, Feeling Good,* and *Divorce Is Not the Answer.* See the bibliography.

If you find your partner caught in the negative cycle, you may be able to break the cycle by asking him to take a break and discuss it later when both of you have had time to cool off.

You might say, "I feel like I am being blamed for hurting you, and I certainly did not want to hurt you, and I do not want you to feel hurt. I would like to go out for a walk with you for about 20 minutes in silence and talk about this when we get back. Will you walk with me?"

Or you might make a similar plan that includes a period of exercise and silence to let the emotions cool down before tackling a further discussion.

Any time you find yourself or your partner in the grip of a negative emotion and you realize this before it gets out of control, take a break. One of the best ways to break up negative thinking is exercise: running, swimming, walking.

Some very effective information can be found in a series of parenting books. The most important of these is *How to Talk so Kids will Listen and How to Listen so Kids will Talk.* It is written as a parenting book, but it is much more than that. The same principals can be applied to any relationship very effectively. This is not to say that you have to treat your partner like a child. These books script respectful relationships with children and are useful in any relationship where we want to generate more peace and understanding. There is a complete list in the Bibliography

3. Toxic anger, rage

Some people have rage stored in them. It might be of deep psychological, psychotic or antisocial proportions. It may be the result of a physical problem or brain injury. Such people become angry with little or no provocation and cannot or will not control themselves. If your partner engages in unprovoked rage and can't or won't control himself, then you must treat this situation very differently from the first two categories above.

For example, a man came home and raged at his wife about the "lousy dinner she made!" In fact, she had made a nice dinner and she was not so emotionally destroyed herself that she didn't know it was a nice dinner. Then he moved on to tell her what a mess the house was, how terrible she looked, and why didn't the children behave. All of this in the face of a nice dinner, a clean house, and a neat wife and reasonably well behaved children.

This woman does not argue back because she knows she is dealing with toxic rage; rage based on some other hurt or event which has nothing to do with the events of the day.

What does she do? There are many appropriate responses; here is one. She listens quietly to his ranting, she acknowledges his anger, but does not feed it by reacting to him. She eases out of the room. If she needs to, she may take her purse, car keys, children and drive away. She may wait at a friend's house until she determines that it is safe to go home. She may decide this by calling on the phone and talking to him to see if he has calmed down. Of, if she decides he is dangerous, she may decide to go to a shelter.

The point is, she does not attempt to take on toxic rage at that moment. This is not something that can be fixed by talking when the partner is raging. *This rage is dangerous, and must be treated as dangerous.*

If you are concerned that your partner suffers from toxic rage, seek counseling from a qualified domestic violence counselor for further ideas about how you can safely address it. If you think you might have problems with your own stored rage—rage from a traumatic childhood, this relationship or other life trauma—consider ways to get help for yourself and, at the same time, continue learning about how to remove yourself from an abusive relationship.

What if I am also abusive?

Many women will look at our list of abusive behaviors and realize that they have done some of the same things. If you think that you are also abusive, acknowledge this. Recognizing your role in this relationship is a major factor. There are two important points to know. First, if you hit him, his response will be to hit you back, and if he is bigger and stronger than you, you do not have a chance. You probably already know this.

Second, while you might be able to stop yourself from your own abusive behavior, you may not be able to stop him. His use of violence is a wrong reaction that he must learn to control. So, while you do not want to contribute to the problem, do not assume your stopping will stop him.

Nevertheless, you can extricate yourself from your own abusive actions by being alert to your behavior, and seeking the help of a trained counselor. It may help if you pull out of the dynamic of abusive behavior.

Chapter 3

What to do next

If you have recognized that your situation is abusive, and you want to change it, your next step is to make a plan.

In most cases, you will want to make both an emergency plan in case an immediate departure is required (Chapter 4), and a longer range plan that might include legal action (Chapters 5 through 14). Ideally, your plan will include alternatives and options: your first and second choices for various steps that you might take.

Your plan should include the following:

✦   Locate a shelter, support group, and counselor (Chapter 5).

✦   Define your informal support group: friends, family, neighbors (Chapter 6).

✦   Consider practical steps you can take to improve your situation (Chapter 7).

✦   Learn local police policies and how to deal with police in your area (Chapter 7)

✦   Consider other women's experiences. See if you can learn anything from members of your support group (Chapter 8).

✦   Review possible legal actions you might take (Chapters 9 through 17).

✦   If legal action is indicated, locate a qualified legal advisor. Contact a domestic violence legal clinic, or a Certified Family Law Specialist experienced in domestic violence issues.

Moving away can require a fair amount of planning, so let's go into that in a little more detail. Go over each step carefully with your counselor, support group, or attorney. For example, let's assume you have already located a shelter, support group, and counselor, and have made plans for an emergency exit if one should be required. Let's say you have also decided that you have to leave the situation entirely. When is the best time? What's the best way to do it?

✦ One woman had to wait until an annual bonus was automatically deposited into a joint bank account so she could withdraw half (her community property share) and go into hiding.

✦ Another had to wait until her husband went on vacation with his girlfriend so she could move her inherited antiques (her separate property) out of the house. She videotaped the entire move to prove exactly what she was taking.

✦ One woman decided she needed to get a job skill before she could leave. The only way she could get out of the house was to skip her hair and nail appointments to take a class, so she did her own hair and nails for a year and he never suspected a thing. Meanwhile, she also gathered documents, made copies and replaced the originals over time. She never knew from one day to the next how long the scheme would last, but she stuck with it and it worked. She completed her computer training, interviewed and got a job before she left. She became so focused and strong in knowing what she wanted that, by the time she left, the relationship had shifted. He became dependent on her emotionally and stopped hitting her. She decided to leave anyway.

✦ Another woman researched financial assistance through the school and discovered that she could leave her husband and go to school on financial assistance.

Circumstances can force you to take immediate action before your plans are complete, but you can always go back to planning from a new location. If you want further help on planning, an excellent book on the subject is *How to Get Control of Your Time and Your Life* (see the bibliography).

PART TWO

HOW TO STOP DOMESTIC VIOLENCE

Chapter 4

Plan for an emergency

People always ask, "What is the first thing I should do?" It will always seem that there are a hundred first things. Use your common sense. If your safety or the safety of the children is threatened, just get away. Drop whatever you were doing and leave. If you have more time, read this book, think and plan.

If your situation is volatile, you may need to leave at any time without much warning. You will feel much better and be much safer if you can be prepared mentally and emotionally to leave if you have to. Take the time to do some emergency planning. Do it right away; start now.

Here is a list of practical suggestions that will make an emergency departure easier, safer and more effective. If you can't complete all of these, never mind; do what you can, as soon as you can. If the need arises, get away with what you've got.

1. Get an extra set of car keys made. Keep them with a friend or at work. You will use these to get the car. Later, if you also get a court order that you can keep the car, you can consider having the ignition lock and door locks changed. Consider keeping the car off the street and away from places he frequents.

2. Memorize important phone numbers. Leave a written set with a friend or in a secure place at work. Your list might include numbers for a shelter, a domestic violence counselor, your children's school and favorite friends, your own friends or relatives—people you can call and places you can go in an emergency.

3. Memorize how to get to a shelter or other safe place. Understand what a truly "safe place" is. It is not your sister's house if he knows where she lives and is likely to think you will go there. It is a place where he cannot find you. You must remove yourself from his orbit. Stores, banks, shops, bars he frequents are off limits. Think this through carefully with a support person.

4. Gather important records, and keep copies in a safe place, such as a friend's house or at work. Here is a checklist of some of the documents you may need:

+ Birth certificates for you and the children

+ A copy of his birth certificate

+ Your social security card and cards for the children (if any)

+ His social security number

+ Your driver's license

+ His driver's license number

+ A photo of him

+ Photos of the children

+ A description of his car, a description of your car, auto license number, copy of registration and insurance information

+ School records

+ Money

+ Bankbooks

+ Credit cards

+ Keys for your house, car, office

+ Welfare identification

+ Immigration papers

+ Visa

+ Passport

+ Green card

+ Work permit

✦ Divorce papers

✦ House deed, lease, rental agreement

✦ Mortgage payment book

✦ Current bills

✦ Insurance papers

✦ Marriage certificate

✦ Copies of court orders against him, if there are any

5. Put emergency clothes for you and the children somewhere safe where you can pick them up if you have to leave without having time to pack.

6. Get a mail box. You may need to move around until you get settled and this will help you stabilize your personal business affairs. Try to find a mail box service with a street address, because court forms can't be mailed to a PO box..

7. Get an answering service. This will increase your stability if you are going to change jobs or look for work.

8. Apply for a credit card in your own name, using your mail box address.

9. Make a checklist of items you will want to take with you if you have to leave quickly and begin packing away some those items or put them in a place where they can be packed quickly. Move some of them out of the house discreetly. Here are some items you may want on your list:

✦ Keys

✦ Clothes

✦ Medications

✦ Address book

✦ Pictures

✦ Jewelry

✦ Photos

✦ Mementos

✦ Children's favorite toys and/or favorite blanket

Whatever you leave behind, you may never see again. This is both painful and liberating. Plan with this understanding, then if you later are able to regain tangible possessions, so much the better.

> "But all of a sudden, as I looked around the house, I realized that everything was . . . replaceable except me. So I took my little dog, and I left. It was raining outside. It was December. My heart was pounding, and, oh, my adrenaline must have been going crazy. As I was going out, I saw my husband and his friend coming toward the apartment, but they didn't see me, so I turned and went the other way. I walked in the rain with my dog . . . all the way downtown. . . . The next morning, I flew back to my parents' home." (Excerpt from *The Battered Woman.*)

If there comes a time when you have to choose between safety and life over possessions, it is better to be prepared mentally in advance.

10. Alert the children's school if you have an order restraining him from coming near them. Give a certified copy to the school administration and teachers. Be sure the school knows exactly who is permitted to pick the children up.

11. Open a bank account at a bank away from the one he uses.

12. If you stay in the home and he leaves or is removed, secure your home.

✦ Change the locks and put secure locks on all doors and windows

✦ Install security devices

✦ Get a guard dog

✦ Close the drapes at night

✦ Check the fences, gates, locks

✦ Have someone move in with you

✦ Warn the neighbors

✦ Change your phone to an unlisted number

✦ Screen your calls with an answering machine

13. Ask the neighbors to be on alert and call 911 if they hear sounds of violence from your home.

Chapter 5

Locate a shelter, a support group, a counselor

Once you have done some emergency planning, the single most important step you can take is to get help from the right people. A drowning man can't be saved by someone who can't swim. You need expert advice by a trained person. Here are some suggestions on how to find the right counselor. What you are going to do now is build a new support network.

Battered women's shelters and temporary emergency housing

Most battered women's shelters* are an excellent source of reliable information and referrals to counselors who are trained in domestic violence. Do not be put off by the word "shelter"; these agencies offer a wide range services at no charge to you. In addition to safe housing, they often have support groups and counseling services. Find one near you, and find out what they offer. For leads to a shelter near you, call the police or a social service agency in your community. Even if the closest shelter is not in your town, establish a telephone consultation arrangement and visit the shelter if you can.

The temporary emergency housing provided by these shelters is confidential. If you move temporarily to a shelter, you will not be required to disclose your address or telephone number to any person or agency.

---

* When Dr. Lenore Walker wrote her book in 1979, there were about 60 battered women's shelters in the United States by her count. At this writing in 1995, there are at least 60 centers and shelters for battered women in Los Angeles County alone. We have come a long way. There is a world of help out there. Use it.

There might be people in the shelter more distressed than you. They can be disturbing, but sometimes you can learn something from them. If you don't like the shelter, at least you can be safe there long enough to find another one, or create a more suitable safe haven for yourself somewhere else.

The key to a safe haven is that you are safe. You do not answer the phone, you do not come to the door, and you do not park on the street. You live there anonymously. You do not get mail there. Of course you do not disclose your address or telephone number to *anyone*. There is no need; *you* call *them;* or they can leave a message with your message service.

Memorize the address of the nearest shelter now and how to get there.

How to find a shelter near you

There are so many shelters and hotline numbers in California, and they change so often, that it is not possible to keep an up-to-date list. Here are a few ways to find a shelter near you:

Ask the police. If there is an emergency, call 911. When the police respond, whatever else they do, they will refer you to the nearest shelter. State law requires this.

If there is no emergency, call or stop by the local police station and ask for their list of local domestic violence services. If they don't have one, they are in violation of state law. Penal Code § 13701 requires that they give you a written list of shelters in your area.

The phone book. Call information and ask for domestic violence hotlines or services in your area. Ask for a child abuse hotline if children are involved. In Los Angeles County, call the Domestic Violence Safety Plan Hotline 1-800-978-3600. Look in the phone book under Women's Centers, Domestic Violence, Spousal Abuse, Women's Shelters, Battered Women's Shelters, or Legal Aid.

Libraries, legal aid, clerk's office. Many public libraries, law libraries and legal aid clinics keep lists of shelters and hotlines in your area. The Superior Court Clerk's office at the courthouse may have a list of resources and services, some of which may even operate through the court.

Domestic violence counseling

After you find a shelter, get a referral to a domestic violence counselor. This is a therapist or other person who is specially trained in domestic violence counseling. This person can help you assess your situation and develop a plan. Often the volunteers at the shelters are the best informed and can give excellent practical advice. If you can't afford private counseling, there are literally hundreds of counseling agencies in this state that offer free or sliding-scale counseling services. Ask for a referral to one of these.

Support groups

If at all possible, attend a domestic violence support group. The shelter will probably offer one or refer you to any in the area. A support group is made up of a trained group leader and other women from abusive relationships. The purpose of the group is to be supportive to each woman as she works out a solution to overcome the violence in her life. Try not judge the other women if any of them seem to be in bad shape. The group can help you and you can help others in the group, simply by being there and by being open.

Legal advice and domestic violence law clinics

Get competent and complete legal advice. Locate a domestic violence law clinic. These clinics are set up to help you through the process of obtaining a restraining order. They often have family law attorneys associated with them who can give you excellent advice. If there is no clinic in your area, look for one in a town nearby.

You do not have to retain an attorney. It is possible to handle your own case and never speak to an attorney. However, if you have questions you want answered or if certain issues have you bewildered, get a consultation with an attorney who is a State Bar Certified Family Law Specialist (CFLS) and who is also experienced in domestic violence.

You can limit the cost of your case if you simply hire an attorney for a consultation on an hourly basis to review your plans and let you know if you are on the right track. If you have significant property, health problems or child custody issues, get that consultation right away. Get it before you act.

Ask local shelters if they can refer you to a qualified attorney. Also ask your counselor and speak to members of your support group. Look at the list of resources in the back of this book for further contacts. Interview several attorneys. Don't be shy about asking questions about their qualifications. Find one who is qualified that you like.

Other groups: 12-step and substance abuse

If you or your mate have a substance abuse problem, get into a 12-step program or other substance abuse program. You need as many support structures around you as you can build. AA was created initially for alcoholics, but it also serves for any substance abuse. Al-Anon was created for families of alcoholics to help them cope with the addicted person's behavior. These groups are anonymous and include a mentor program. Some women attend meetings five times a week to stay in a supportive environment. Try going to some meetings; try different groups; then decide.

Growing pains

So now you are thinking, "All these new people and new ideas in my life; my head is spinning." Indeed. You are changing your life. In the past you have been surrounded by a family and other social structures that supported or tolerated your abuse. Now, as you go from violence toward the goal of peace at home, much will change. Everything will feel different, a little funny. If you feel like you are being uprooted, it is because you are. If not physically, then emotionally. Don't be afraid, don't worry; your feeling of disorientation will gradually diminish.

While all this change is coming at you, stay in the driver's seat. Hear the advice, listen to the input, sift it around, then make your own decisions. Only *you* know your exact situation. You may not be able to articulate to others all the details of what you are facing. Don't let others make decisions for you; don't give up your regained power to these new people. Just listen to them. Take in as much as you can, then decide what is best for you.

Chapter 6

Informal support: Family, friends and neighbors

How to use informal support

Now you have a shelter, a counselor and a support group. These are the qualified people who understand how to handle domestic violence; you will use them to help you make a plan to deal with the abuse in your life.

Friends, family and neighbors can help you in other ways. For example, you need someone who will store your emergency kit. These people do not need to be experts in domestic violence, they just need to be people you can trust.

Use your friends and family for emotional support, distraction, favors. A friend might be willing to pick up a child from school. A neighbor might be willing to call the police if they sense trouble at your house. Friends can go to a movie with you or help in a million ways that do not require training and experience in domestic violence.

Many people in your life will be eager to give you advice; it's a way of being close with you, a way to be important. Always listen politely, thank them sincerely for their concern, but do *not* take their advice to heart. It is not fair to them or you. They aren't trained in domestic violence, they don't know enough about it, they have their own agendas. Stick to expert advice. You don't have to tell them this, just do it.

If you have a friend, relative or neighbor who is willing to help you, ask them to read Appendix A so they will better understand the issues of domestic violence and what you are facing.

Who can you use for informal support?

Your minister, maybe

Some ministers believe that the marriage is more important than the personal safety of the wife. Some do not believe that it is wrong for a man to hit his wife or children. Sometimes it takes a woman many years to leave an abusive relationship because she has been taught that it is not wrong for a man to hit his wife. If you do not know where your church or minister stands on these issues, find out, and act accordingly. Make some indirect inquiries and have someone ask if the minister is trained in domestic violence counseling. Some are. If so, your minister may be of great assistance to you. If not, stay clear.

Church social services

Some churches have social services. For example, in Los Angeles, Catholic Charities, and Jewish Community Centers offer extensive social services. They may have shelters and trained counselors. Ask them.

Your family, maybe

In some families, spousal abuse is accepted. Sometimes the family is not as supportive as you need them to be for their own personal reasons. Do not assume that your relatives will side with you. Find out as discreetly as you can where your family members stand and what their ideas are about domestic abuse.

Therapists, maybe

A therapist who is not trained and experienced in domestic violence can be dangerous. They may have an agenda for saving the relationship and they almost certainly don't know enough about the realities of domestic violence. It is important to get your advice about domestic abuse from someone who is trained and experienced in it.

Police, maybe

Some police departments are well trained in domestic violence and are of great assistance to distressed families; other departments are not. Find out what your local police policies are. The shelters will certainly know the police practices in local areas. Ask them. Go to the station and ask what kind of help they offer. After you find out, continue to expect nothing. Make your plans independent of police assistance. Then, if they help you, so much the better. See Chapter 7 for more about how to get the police on your side.

Checklist for your support network

1. Do you have a qualified domestic violence counselor?

2. Are you seeing your counselor once a week?

3. Do you have contact with a battered women's shelter?

4. Are you in a battered women's support group?

5. Are you attending as often as you can?

6. Have you reviewed your plans with your counselor, your support group?

7. Can you rely on your minister for help?

8. What private social services does your church offer?

9. Can you rely on family members for help? Who? What help?

10. Are there neighbors, friends, co-workers who will help? Who? What kind of help?

11. What are the local police policies on domestic violence?

12. Do you have a family law specialist attorney you can consult who is versed in domestic violence?

Chapter 7

Practical advice

There are some practical steps you can take to begin to improve your situation and protect yourself. A few are listed below. With the help of an experienced domestic violence counselor, you may be able to work out more options and practical solutions specifically tailored to your situation.

Tell him to stop! Exactly what to say

You can tell him to stop the abusive behavior and mean it. Some abusers stop when they are challenged and told to stop. You can use your own words, but it may help to go over our script. Work on it with a trusted friend. Practice it. Role play.

Tell him exactly what he has done. For example,

> "When you called me a fat bitch in front of your friend, that was destructive and disrespectful to me."

Then tell him to stop. Say

> "That is unacceptable to me. I will not tolerate it. Do not ever do that again."

There's no need to threaten him with what you will do if he doesn't stop. Just draw the line and explain exactly what he can't do.

Some people respond to definite limits. You will be surprised at how effective this can be. Role play with a friend and work on it until you have it down, then use it with him. Even if you feel you didn't do it well at first or sound confident, keep trying. The message is what counts.

Expose him

Sometimes, when a batterer is exposed or fears exposure, he stops. A classic example of this is documented in Del Martin's book *Battered Wives*. He published a letter from a woman who had endured many savage beatings by her wealthy, prominent doctor husband. She finally came up with a plan to stop it. She wrote a letter describing her beatings and exactly what her husband had done to her. She sent this letter to key people. She asked them to send this letter to the police and other important people if anything ever happened to her.

She then told her husband what she had done. According to Del Martin, the husband never laid a finger on her again.

Protect your space

If you need to remain in the home and want him to leave, ask him to leave. Some abusers will actually go if asked. If he won't leave and you aren't ready to file for a Domestic Violence Restraining Order, take practical steps to protect your space.

Stay out of enclosed spaces with him. Consider moving into another bedroom; put a lock on the door and install a telephone in your room. Can you avoid being home alone with the abusive person? Rearrange your work hours?

Consider bringing in a family member or roommate to live with you, at least temporarily. Researchers tell us that domestic violence is dramatically reduced when a third adult is present.

Ask for what you want or need

Sometimes the abuser wants an end to the situation as much as you do. Researchers tell us the battered woman and her man often have very poor verbal communication. Have you ever simply stated exactly what you want in a clear, concise statement? Think about it. If not, try it.

Write down what you want, practice telling it to a friend until you can deliver your message in simple, clear terms. If he is willing to move, ask him also for custody of the children, use of the car, and whatever else you need. You may be on a roll. Some men will agree.

When you think about it, you will know better than anyone what you can ask for. Even if he does not agree, you will find out how serious he is about remaining with you or fighting for custody of the children and so on.

See what issues you can work out peacefully. Do not push it, but see what he will agree to do. Even if he later changes his mind, you will have started a pattern of peaceful resolution. He may flip back and forth several times before you have resolved things. Just keep focused on your goals, and calmly work toward them. If he will agree, get to an attorney, have the agreement written up, and have him sign it.

Be alert. Avoid what sets him off

Granted, unpredictability is a large factor in many batterer's behavior, but you may know what triggers some of his tirades. Try to avoid circumstances and behavior that sets him off. It is not suggested that you plan to live in a state of high alert forever. This is a just temporary way to get enough peace to make a longer-range plan and complete it. Be practical. For example, if you already know that asking him to leave or asking him to give you custody of the children will produce a violent rage, then this is not your approach.

Build your case

You may never have to go to court, but be prepared anyway. It is very important to have your facts and documents available in case you do have to go to court.

Medical reports. If you are hit or harmed, get a medical examination and treatment whether or not you think it is strictly necessary. Be sure to get a copy of the medical report. Be aware, however, that there is a mandatory reporting law for doctors. If a physician suspects that your injury is the result of abusive behavior or a lethal weapon, the physician is required to report the injury to the police. Some physicians are not aware of these laws, so do not assume a report will be made. Tell the doctor to make a report if that's what you want.

Since your visit to a doctor could trigger a police action, read the section in Chapter 7 and be prepared for it.

Police reports. Call the police and make a report; be sure to get a copy of the report. Read the section below about how to deal with police.

Photograph injuries and property damage. Even though the police are required to gather evidence and photograph your injuries, these photos may not be made available to you when you need them, so get your own photos made as well. Take them the day of the incident and take more every few days if more bruises emerge. Take photos of any property that may have been damaged by the abuser. Keep the negatives in a very safe place and make copies for the police if they want them.

Gather documents, receipts. Keep receipts for all medical expenses, attorney fees, costs, moving and rental expenses if you are forced to move as a result of the abusive behavior. If you need child support, gather documents of his income. If you cannot get these, consider subpoenaing his payroll records (see Appendix C). Also gather information about his assets and debts. For example, make copies of his pay stubs, bank records and tax returns, and return the originals. Be prepared to prove his income, your income, what it costs you to live, what debts and special needs you and he have.

Keep a diary. Make a diary or log of every incident. Note the date and time and describe what happened. If there were witnesses, keep track of their full names, addresses, and telephone numbers. Ask them to give you a statement under penalty of perjury. See Chapter 16E for the proper form and instructions. If you can't get a formal declaration, then a signed letter stating that "the above facts are true under penalty of perjury under the laws of the state of California" will do.

Get a restraining order

If it appears that an intolerable situation is going to continue, consider getting a restraining order. Read Parts 3 and 4. A restraining order can be very effective when used along with the other practical steps discussed in this book.

For example, one woman, who was living with her abusive boyfriend and their child, decided as part of her plan to get a restraining order while they were still living together. He was required to move his bedroom and office downstairs and was restrained from yelling at her and having any physical contact with her. He was permitted to continue living in her home, and was permitted to care for the child while she worked, but he was not permitted to come within five yards of her, call her at work, or harass her in any way. He was also prohibited from removing their child from Los Angeles County. After several weeks, she reported that he was furious that the order had been made, but it was working.

Domestic violence laws were made to protect you. Learn about them, and use them if it seems appropriate.

How to get the police on your side

Police are required by law to enforce domestic violence laws and to have clearly stated policies for dealing with these cases. Call your local police agency and find out what their policies are. They should have a public or community relations officer who can give you complete policy information and available brochures with referral information.

If you feel you need police help, don't hesitate to ask for it. Whenever you make statements about abuse, be completely truthful and accurate. Do not exaggerate or minimize. Never, never tell one story to the police and another to the court or to friends or anyone. Inconsistent stories will probably come back to haunt you later.

If it is not an emergency, but you have been threatened, injured, or harassed, call the police or go to the police station and make a report to document the incident. They are required by law to take the report. If there is property damage or you have visible injuries, make sure it is all photographed.

In an emergency, call 911. Tell the dispatcher you are in danger and need help. Explain the situation; if you have a restraining order, tell them. Ask for the dispatcher's name and ID number and note the time of your call. If the police do not respond quickly, call again and tell them it is your second call.

When the police arrive, tell them specifically what the abuser did—not a long story about your entire relationship, just what he did this time. If you have visible injuries, make sure they are described and photographed. If you have a restraining order, tell them about it, show them a copy of it and the proof of service if you have one. Describe your injuries. Ask them to file a report and give you the report number. If appropriate, ask them to help you get an Emergency Protective Order (EPO). Write down the name and badge number of each officer.

Arrest on the scene. If the police observe fresh injuries to *either* party, the other party might be arrested and taken to jail (so, if the abuser is injured, you could be taken in.) If you are afraid the abuser will come back and hurt you unless they take him into custody, say so. If you want the abuser arrested and they refuse, tell them you want to make a citizens' arrest. Assure them you will follow through. If he is taken into custody, he could be released in a few hours. Use this time wisely. Either get to a safer place, or have an EPO issued, or both.

Children on the scene. Police have the power to remove children and place them in temporary foster care, but they will only do so if it looks like the children are in danger, or not being cared for, or if the mother appears unable to care for them. If your children are at the scene, show the police that you are able to take care of them. Cooperate with their suggestions. If you are asked to keep the abuser out of the house, agree and really do it. If they suggest you have the children stay with someone else for a few days, until things settle down, agree and arrange to have a friend or relative come and pick them up. You can bring them back later.

Understand their view. Police are injured more often in domestic cases than in almost any other line of their work. They are frustrated by the fact that so many women don't follow through, who later refuse to press charges or testify, who let the abuser back in their lives to start the cycle all over again. It is not uncommon for police to arrest the abuser only to get resistance from the victim. Police feel uncomfortable getting in the middle of dysfunctional domestic relationships.

How to get the police on your side. Always be straight, tell things exactly as they happened, and follow through. If you don't like the way they are acting, stay civil and tell them what you think is right and fair. Never get nasty or difficult; police talk among themselves and you may want police help again some day.

Get a restraining order! This is the very best way to get police on your side. It is one of the best reasons for getting a restraining order. It shows them that you are serious about not being a victim, willing to take steps and follow through. They know you are serious. Besides, police are required by law to enforce restraining orders. When you have a restraining order, they *have* to be on your side.

Things to avoid

Do not expect to change him

This does not mean that you are to blame for the abuse or that you have "brought it on yourself." That is not the point. The abuse is the fault of the abuser. Violence, control, threats and intimidation are tools he uses to get what he wants. The point is that what you do can make a difference.

Changing yourself means that you take your power back. The abusive person may seem very large and strong and powerful to you at the beginning of this process. One of the reasons this person seems so big is that you believe in him. You have given him his power over you. Another reason he may seem so big is that you may have lost your self worth, and therefore you feel small. He may also be physically bigger.

However, as you regain your personal power, your perception of him will change. He will seem to shrink and you will begin to see him in a more neutral light, for what he really is. He may appear more like an insecure bully; or an immature boy in a man's body; or he may appear ill; whatever. He will seem less powerful, less dominating. This will come in time, but do not force it or try to rush the process. Just notice it when it does come. You will also see your fear shrinking.

At the same time, he may still be dangerous. Do not lose sight of this. Try to operate from an attitude of practical, healthy fear, not paralysis.

Do not go to counseling with him

If your partner is physically abusive or subject to violent rages, do not expect to get him into traditional counseling. Do not try to get him into joint marriage counseling or individual therapy. You should even refuse to go to traditional counseling with him. Your desire to change him is part of his power to control you and is based on the myth that you can affect his behavior. He will only change when he decides to do so; you can't do it for him and you can't count on being able to help him decide to change. Research and experience show that this is a bad bet.

Joint counseling is for partners who are mutually interested in a balanced relationship. If one person lives in fear and intimidation, balance is not possible.

Things to do

Ask for a court-approved program for batterers

Court-approved counseling programs for batterers begin with a session in which the victim is alone with the batterer's counselor and explains what is happening in the relationship from her perspective. The parties do not meet together with the counselor. During the program, the counselor will meet with the woman alone from time to time to find out if the batterer is actually improving his behavior.

Study books on domestic violence

Knowledge is power. When you have a greater understanding of what has been happening in your life, you will improve your ability to find help and overcome the abuse. If there are no support groups in your area, find one in another area close to you and ask for referrals to a counselor within your reach. If there is no qualified counselor in your area, find one in a nearby community and have telephone consults, or go to the library and read. Look for the books listed in the bibliography, and if your library does not have them, ask them to get these books. Order them from a bookstore. Become unstoppable.

Going underground—not recommended

There is an underground network that helps women escape from their abuser, either alone or with the children, and go underground. You think, "I am desperate; that sounds like a way out; I'll take the children and leave." Think again.

Running away can lead to a life of constant worry and it may invite criminal penalties if you steal his children. From counseling women who wanted to resurface after having gone underground, we learn that after they take the children, the father usually goes to court and gets an order granting him custody. When she is served with these orders, if the woman does not immediately return to court or return the children, she will be in violation of a court order and may be incurring criminal liability as well.

An even bigger problem arises when the woman tires of running and wants to get her true identity and life back. The woman has a harder time straightening out the custody issue and the children now have to go through another identity change.

Do everything you can before you consider an underground life. It will only lead to a life of constant stress and worry for both you and the children. Find another way to solve your problems. Read this book, get into a support group, and get advice from a qualified domestic violence counselor.

Chapter 8

Four stories of domestic violence

Elisa

Elisa had been married to her abuser for five years. At the time they separated, he was working a lot of overtime under threat of losing his job and, if that happened, he wouldn't be able to support his parents any longer. He became more and more angry. In his relationship with Elisa, he went from yelling and swearing to breaking things. He pushed Elisa around and, more recently, he got drunk and hit her. His bad behavior often took place in the presence of the children. She asked him to leave and he moved to his parent's house. Elisa had previously separated from him several times under similar circumstances. When he moved out the last time, the children were ages three and one.

Both spouses had a pension plan, and they owned one car. He took it. Her salary was not enough to support herself and the children and, although he made three or four times her salary, he was not supporting them at all. They were about to receive a settlement of $20,000 from a lawsuit. She did not believe he was an alcoholic, but he had become more irresponsible and was drinking more. And he owned a gun.

Elisa was able to get her abusive husband to move out voluntarily, but she still had to go to court on an emergency basis to get orders that restrained him from bothering her, granted her child custody and half the funds from the lawsuit, and required him to stay away from the family home and pay child support. She did not want the use of the car. She also got an order that he was to surrender his gun to the police, which he did.

Once she had her temporary orders, they worked out a visitation plan and filed it with the court. After several months, her father talked to both of them, and they reconciled. This reconciliation has lasted seven years to date. I asked her what made this reconciliation work. She said that her father talked to each of them alone. She never found out what he told her husband, but he told her how important family was and that she had to learn to deal with her husband. He suggested that she tell her husband two things:

a. You support your wife and children first. We come first, then you can contribute to the support of your parents.

b. Do not ever hit me again. Do not raise your voice and do not throw things. It is improper behavior, and it is damaging to the children. I will not tolerate this behavior and my family will not tolerate this behavior.

She had never done this before; she had never told him what she expected. After she said these things, he moved home overjoyed and relieved to be out from under the assignment of his wages for support. He remains very clear on what he can and cannot do; he has settled down and reduced his drinking.

Elisa had never gotten court orders before. This shocked and confused him. He was stunned that the court could take part of his wages for family support, order him to stay away, and that the court could give her part of the funds coming from the lawsuit.

The point of this example is that some men will respond when clear limits are set. Also, temporary orders snap some men out of outrageous behavior.

Delia

Delia was married to her wealthy executive husband for two years. At the time she decided to leave, he was 45 and she was 30. She was partially handicapped by a rare spinal disorder. This disability flared up during the marriage and she was obliged to quit her job. It affected her ability to walk or stand for long periods of time. Later, when she felt ready to find part-time work, he discouraged her. At first, she thought he was being protective.

She had noticed that he was somewhat obsessive prior to the marriage. After the marriage, after she lost her job, he became extreme. He attempted to control her every move. He did not want her to work and made that clear. He checked up on her. They lived near his office, and he insisted on taking her to lunch every day and then to dinner. At first it was fun, but then she realized he was obsessed and would not let her out of his sight. She felt like a French poodle. She felt that she could not do anything and what she did attempt, he criticized and belittled. She tried to cook, but he was so critical that she gave it up. She tried to paint and he reduced her to emotional immobility. His rages began to increase.

He was also obsessed with pornography and insisted that she watch pornographic videos with him. He began to push her around and at Christmas he pushed her into the Christmas tree, knocking them both over. He was immediately filled with remorse and campaigned to win her back. She was not in a position to do much else, so she stayed.

At this point, she realized he was dangerous. With her physical disorder, that kind of fall could have killed her. She decided to explore leaving. They each had a car from prior to the marriage. She had one joint credit card, and her name was on a joint account. He had accumulated some pension deposits during the marriage, but she had been able to accumulate nothing. There were a few credit card debts, but nothing significant. Her furniture was in the apartment which they rented along with a few things they acquired together and a few of his personal things.

Delia located a battered women's shelter and got counseling there. She was referred to and joined a support group. It was a real eye-opener for her. She began to realize more about her situation. It fit a pattern.

She started looking for an attorney to learn what she could do. She found a Certified Specialist, and made sure the attorney was experienced in domestic violence actions. She made a plan and reviewed it with the attorney, the support group and several volunteers at the shelter. She decided to have her three brothers come from out of state to help her move. She wanted to take what belonged to her and have no confrontation. She knew this would mean she would have to live a double life for a few months, but she felt it was the price she would have to pay.

She began packing her smaller things and moving them out of the apartment. She began gathering records and making copies. She was careful not to take anything that did not belong to her and she was careful to return all original documents. She did not want to treat her husband unfairly, she just wanted to get away from his unreasonable behavior.

She had to wait until her husband's annual bonus was deposited into the joint account, so she planned to move the day after the deposit was made. On that day, the van and her brothers arrived half an hour after her husband left for work; later, she called and cancelled lunch with him. She was able to pack, load and move out all her things by 2:00 p.m.

She went to the bank and removed funds equal to half the accumulated community property. She left him a letter explaining exactly what she had done and why. She wanted him to understand what funds she had taken and her logic.

She then moved to an undisclosed residence out of state. For several months, she had a mail box with a street address and an answering service. When the case was resolved and all accounts settled, she terminated these.

On the day she moved, her attorney filed papers for dissolution and for temporary orders for support, use of the funds she took with her, and exclusive use of her furniture and household possessions. She fully explained her move to the Court in her papers. Her husband was served with papers the next day.

Once her husband's behavior was made public, and after his initial reaction of rage, he realized that the game was over. He was a very intelligent businessman and responded to her fair division of the funds with a reasonable settlement offer to conclude the case. She returned once to California to attend the hearing. On this day, she and her attorney met with him and his attorney at the court house and resolved the rest of the case peacefully. When the case was settled, both parties indicated they felt the settlement was fair, and they parted on relatively friendly terms.

There are several valuable lessons to be learned from Delia's story. Even though hers was a divorce action, all of the orders she applied for could be applied for in a domestic violence case, except for spousal support. Her planning is a good model. She was careful to get good advice. She was careful to take only those things which were hers. Before leaving, she was careful to leave all original documents and make only copies. She took only those funds she was lawfully entitled to and she played fair. She had the documents to prove this. She timed her departure, the removal of the funds, and her move to minimize the chance of confrontation, hostility and violence. She had a strong support group with her the day of the move: three supportive, understanding brothers. Most important, she had been careful to find supportive and informed people to help her plan. She did not talk about her plan to anyone other than the support people who needed to know. Her plan worked very smoothly because she stuck to it and because she kept checking and updating it along the way.

Helen

Helen was married to her abuser for fifteen years at the time she decided to leave. She was actually still living with him after they were divorced and he had already transferred all of the property into her name. They had a six-year-old daughter.

Helen was pushed around, hit, dragged across the floor and generally abused for the last five years they were together. She left him several times and went to a shelter with her daughter. Two years previously, he was able to get her to come home because he went to court and obtained a temporary emergency custody order granting him custody of the minor child when Helen and the child were living in the shelter. The court ordered that Helen return the child to him. She had no choice. She came home with the child and his custody order expired. She felt trapped.

The violence started again. He told her that the property he put in her name was all his. He is a lawyer; he convinced her that he could legally get it back from her. He also told her that if she would not sign it back to him, he would kill her and take it back. She believed he would do it. He threatened to kill her parents. Her parents had seen him threaten a process server with a gun and they were afraid of him even though they live in a far-off state. She sought legal advice on several occasions, but was so paralyzed with fear that she could not act. During the time she stayed, the abuse continued.

When he attempted to force her to sign the documents deeding the house back to him, she refused. He attacked her. She escaped with her daughter and some cash and went into hiding. She stayed with a relative for a few days, then moved into an apartment in another city. She filed for custody and had him served.

She applied for a visitation plan that provided a neutral drop-off place halfway between the two cities, at a restaurant, and took a support person with her each time. She arranged not to be alone with him for many months, but he eventually found out where she lived.

He pressured her into signing over the property to him. She valued her life over the property and felt that if she gave in, she could be free of him. She was able to keep custody of her daughter and gained the court's permission to move away to a more remote city. He requested a child custody evaluation, which showed the mother to be the more stable and nurturing parent. She eventually moved to an even more distant city and began her life over.

It took Helen many tries before she finally was able to get away. She only left when she was forced to. She left almost everything behind and took only some cash. She kept the bank accounts but gave up all the property. If she could have overcome her fear, she could have kept at least half of the property. Her husband was a scary man. He was big, loud, outrageous and out of control. Yet, she did prevail. She was able to get custody of her daughter and permission from the court to move away. Helen's case shows us that it can be done; you can get your life back.

Martha

Martha had been married to her abusive husband for twenty years. She had two children, ages twelve and fifteen. She and her husband owned a competitive racing bicycle business; both children were involved in the sport and helped with the business.

Her husband was from a culture in which men rule the house and women are treated like property. When Martha married him, he was dashing, romantic, and full of ambition. At the time she decided to leave, he was simply brutal and dangerous. She had been beaten severely many times. When she decided to leave, she was beyond fear, and this made her very powerful. She decided to divorce him no matter what, and she decided that she would get her half of the property and custody of the children. She also expected she would get two more beatings before she could get out. There was no talking her into practical measures to protect herself. She said, "Either he will kill me, or I will get my settlement and leave." She decided it was worth the risk. She was quite definite about this. She went to an attorney and had an interim agreement drawn up. She took it home and asked him to sign it and leave. He did hit her, but he also signed it and moved out.

Several months later, she had final papers drawn up. She went to the bicycle shop and presented him with a complete settlement agreement and the final judgment. He was again enraged, but he did agree to the settlement and she was free. He took the business; she took the house, children, child support and lifetime support for herself. He was a businessman. Because they lived in a small town, he understood that if she took him to court, the abuse would be revealed, and his business would suffer. He also realized that she was offering a fair settlement.

One year later, she was a new woman; no longer the quiet, gray shadow. Light had returned to her eyes, and color to her whole being. The children were still active with their father's sport and business, but also had built more balanced lives, free of the shadow of their father's domination and brutality. The father was quite subdued. He had lost his prey. He was quiet, reclusive, and treated his employees in an almost kindly way.

Martha was willing to face violent rage and she prevailed. She decided her freedom was worth more than life itself. Her decision to face him alone and stand for her rights was inspiring and yet appalling.

[CAW: Martha was the first battered wife I worked with. It was over twenty years ago in a small town in another state. Hundreds of cases have followed, and I can now think of better, safer ways to walk away from domestic abuse, but I have never forgotten what she faced. She is one reason I have continued to work with battered women. This book is dedicated to her and to the thousands of women like her who struggle to face domestic demons.]

PART THREE

PREPARING FOR LEGAL ACTION

Chapter 9

Emergency action

Leave

If you are attacked, leave if you can and go to a shelter or other safe place. When you are safe, consider your practical options (Chapter 7) and work out a plan. Work with a counselor and a support group. Give serious consideration to getting a restraining order (see Parts Three and Four).

Call the police

If you can't leave, call the police. Try to have your batterer arrested and taken to jail. Policies differ from one department to another. In Los Angeles County, the policy is that if you have a bruise and he doesn't, he will be arrested. If he has a bruise, too, you could also be arrested. If you go to jail, the police may place your children in foster care, and the courts might declare them wards of the court. This is one of many good reasons why you don't want to participate in the violence. Read the section in Chapter 7. Find out about the domestic violence policy of your local police agencies. If you are concerned that he will bail out and come after you, use the time he is in jail to pack up and leave. Seriously consider getting an emergency protective order (below) and a restraining order.

Get an Emergency Protective Order

An Emergency Protective Order (EPO) is a restraining order, valid for only five to seven days, that can be issued on the telephoned request of a law enforcement officer. In every locality, a judicial officer is on duty 24 hours a day to issue EPOs on an emergency basis. If you get the police involved in your case, you can ask them to get you one. This will give you time to make plans, leave, or get longer-lasting restraining orders of your own. Police agencies have different policies as to when they will request an EPO. For example, if there is a superior court within a reasonable distance and if it is open, they may ask you to get your own orders there. They are more likely to get one for you if the need is immediate and outside of court hours. Call your local police and find out what their policy is on helping you to get an EPO.

Get a restraining order

There are two different paths you can take to get a restraining order. In either case, it is possible to get orders very quickly, even without the abuser being present until the time set for a full hearing.

The Domestic Violence Restraining Order (DVRO). When you apply for a DVRO, you can get temporary orders—good until a full hearing about 21 days later—on the same day you file if you get there in the morning. Orders after the hearing are good for three years. This procedure is very fast, once you've filled out the papers. There is no filing fee, it is not very difficult to do, and the courts are prepared to work with you directly without an attorney. This book shows you how to get a DVRO. Using this book, you should be able to get orders in one or two days if you are in a hurry.

Restraining orders in a family action. If you are married to the abuser or have a child with him, you can get restraining orders as part of a family action. "Family action" includes divorce, legal separation nullity, actions for child custody, visitation and support, and paternity. If you start a family action, or have one already pending, you can get permanent orders that last longer on a wider variety of issues. You can also get ex parte temporary orders very quickly.

How to choose. The advantages of each method and how to choose which is best for you is discussed in Chapter 12.

Build your case

Once the emergency is over, you should carefully build your case. How you do this is described in Chapter 7. Even if you decide not to take legal action at this time, you may need to do it some time in the future and will be very glad to have the diaries, photos, documents, witnesses and records all ready to go.

Chapter 10

About the Domestic Violence Restraining Order

Why restraining orders are effective

For a variety of reasons, a restraining order is very effective, especially when used with other steps recommended in this book. A restraining order can have immediate and dramatic effect on even vicious abusers. On the other hand, the effect of a court order on true crazies or habitual criminals is at best uncertain. If nothing else, it will help get the police to take action against the abuser and let the world know you are standing up for yourself.

When you have a restraining order, the power of the court and the police are brought to bear on the abuser. If necessary, the judge can order the abuser to come in (or be brought in), and jail can be imposed for acts in contempt of the court's orders. The police will work for you more actively because you have shown that you are serious about standing up for yourself against the abuser. Also, police are required by law to enforce restraining orders.

Psychology and drama may be the most important forces at work on your behalf. It usually makes a strong impression when the abuser gets handed a legal document with his name on it, and the order comes directly from a judge who orders the abuser to quit or else! The game has been escalated, the stakes are higher; abuse is no longer a good way to let off steam.

Abusers tend to pick on people they perceive as victims, people who seem weak, helpless, unable to strike back. Getting a restraining order changes your own way of thinking so you no longer act like a victim. You have stood up and taken action to make it clear that you will not put up with abuse. It also becomes clear that society will not put up with it, and the law will act to prevent it.

Restraining orders have many teeth, some quite sharp. There is no one single reason why they work, but one or more of them is likely to work for you. Restraining orders can effectively improve the attitude of the victim, intimidate the abuser, and secure the active cooperation of the police.

There are a variety of legal actions that can result in restraining orders. This book is specifically about one that is fast, effective, and relatively simple to get—the Domestic Violence Restraining Order, also known commonly as the DVRO. You can get a very broad range of orders (below) and include protection for yourself, your children, or any member of your immediate family or member of your household if they are also under possible threat of harm from the abuser.

How fast can you get orders?

If you are under an *immediate* threat of physical or emotional harm, you can get most kinds of restraining orders on the same day you file your papers. If you file too late in the day, orders may be issued on the next business day. Go in early, if possible.

These are called "temporary ex parte restraining orders." It is possible, but not likely, that the judge will ask you questions about your situation before orders are issued. This little bit of court activity when you file your papers and get your temporary ex parte orders is called the ex parte hearing.

Temporary. These orders will last only until the date of your hearing, which is normally held within 21 days of the date you file.

Ex parte means that the orders can be issued without hearing from the other side—ex parte. A general rule in law is that no one gets orders made against him or her without having reasonable notice that a legal action is being taken. It's only fair. However, in the case of *ex parte* temporary orders for domestic violence, the notice can be as little as a phone call by 11 am the day before the hearing. If you can give a good reason (fear of harm to you or your children), you can get these temporary orders with no notice to the abuser at all. First thing he knows about it is when someone hands him the court orders.

If you aren't especially afraid of the abuser, if he is more of a bother than a threat, you can ask for limited temporary orders or no orders at all until after the hearing.

The court makes the *ex parte* temporary orders solely on your say-so. If it turns out at the hearing that you can't prove facts sufficient to support the orders you got, you could possibly be ordered to compensate the abuser for out-of-pocket expenses and attorney's fees incurred due to your temporary orders.

Who can be restrained?

The "domestic" part of the DVRO means that you and the abuser must now have a domestic relationship or have had one in the past. You can restrain:

✦ anyone who has ever resided with you regularly—a mate or roommate

✦ someone you now date or have ever dated

✦ someone you are engaged to or have been engaged to

✦ a spouse or a former spouse

✦ someone you have had a child with

✦ a family member by blood or by marriage

The kinds of orders you can get

A court can make a wide range of orders in a DVRO action. The orders can protect you and any other named person who is in your household.

At your ex parte hearing (when you first file your papers) you can get:

✦ a stay-away order keeping him away from you (over 100 yards)

✦ an order that he not call, contact, annoy, molest, or bother you

✦ an order that he not attack, strike, or threaten you

✦ a kick-out order, removing him from your house (see Chapter 11–6)

✦ an order restraining him from taking the children away from you, or out of the county, or out of the state of California

✦ orders for custody of the children (Chapter 11–2)

✦ orders for visitation—plain or restricted (see Chapter 11–3)

✦   an order granting you exclusive use of a dwelling, car or other property

✦   an order that he surrender his gun to the police and not buy another

If necessary to protect you, he can be ordered not do any other kind of behavior that can be specifically described.

If you are married, he can be restrained from selling, mortgaging, concealing, giving away or damaging community property.

These orders can be obtained with little or no notice to him. They last until the hearing.

At the formal hearing, for which the abuser must be given formal notice—that is, he must be personally served with papers—the court can make orders that will last for up to three years. These orders can include any of the above orders.

In addition, he can be ordered to:

✦   pay you child support

✦   pay you restitution for expenses he caused you for medical care, lost wages, property damage and temporary housing

✦   participate in counseling (you, too, can be ordered to get counseling, but not with him)

✦   pay your attorney's fees and court costs (if you lose, you could be ordered to pay his fees)

✦   pay specified bills

✦   have his wages assigned to cover child support payments

Mutual orders—that is, orders that the parties are not to abuse one another—cannot be issued in your case unless both parties personally appear before the court and present evidence of domestic violence.

Chapter 11

What to do about children, support, property, and other legal issues

1. Who will take care of the children? Child custody orders

When you apply for the DVRO you can request orders that will grant you custody of the children with arrangements for visitation to him. The visitation can be normal, monitored, or have other restrictions placed on it. It is also possible to leave the children with him and have specific visitation orders made for you.

Below, we examine several common options to use as examples, but these are not the only possibilities. Whatever your needs, you can create a plan that works for you.

Leaving the children behind

Some women leave the home and leave the children behind. They believe the abuser will not hurt the children and that, while he will not pay child support to her, he will take care of the children financially if they are with him. They think they will get custody of the children later, after things settle down and they have a stable place for them.

They may be right. However, if he has been violent toward you, or yelled at you in the presence of the children, think again. It is damaging to a child to witness abusive behavior. When you are gone, he may take his anger out on the children or another woman in the presence of the children, and you may end up paying him child support on top of it. If you are not there to protect them, who will? Furthermore, he will control your visitation with the children, and will attempt to control you in this way.

Consider this: if you leave the children behind, it may be very difficult to regain custody of them at a later date. On the other hand, if he has already turned the children against you, or you do not want to live with them, then leaving them behind may be your best course.

If you leave the children with him, you can request an order for visitation. An example of such an order is at Chapter 15C, Order 1: Children left behind.

Taking the children with you

You can leave and take the children with you to some safe haven or to a temporary shelter. If you remove the children from his custody, you *must* request an order for legal and physical custody of the children. Without this, he can go to court and get custody before you do, and he can do this without notice to you because he can't find you. This is what happened in Helen's case, above. Don't let this happen to you. Apply immediately for your custody orders.

Staying in the home with the children

You can request an order from the court that he be removed from the home and that you remain in the home with the children. This is called a "kick-out" order and is discussed in more detail in Section 6, "What to do about your residence." You may need to do this to keep the children in the same school. If you fear that notice of your legal action will provoke an attack or theft of the children, this order can be applied for without notice to him.

Staying in the home with the children and the abuser

You can request an order that you remain in the home with the children and your spouse is restrained even though he stays in the home. If your abuser is not physically violent and you think he will be impressed by a court order and follow it, the court may issue a stay-away order which permits him to remain in the home. He might move into some other room but still use the kitchen and share a bathroom or other specified parts of the house. He can be ordered to stay away from you and to use common facilities at specific times. These orders are useful if the abuser does not have any place to go and the court is reluctant to remove him for this reason. However, if there is physical violence, substance abuse, or any of the other aggravated behaviors, do not try this. Ask for an order that he be completely removed from the house. The court should not hesitate under such circumstances.

Child stealing

Make sure that all your orders provide that he cannot remove the children from their home, change their residence, or remove them from your county (or region or state—define the area that serves the children).

Often, the batterer threatens to steal the children. If this is a real threat, ask the court to order him to deliver the children's passports to you. There are state laws, federal laws, and international treaties that make child stealing a serious crime. If this happens to you, call the police and the DA, and get qualified legal advice on how to enforce your order.

2. Child custody

Terms used in orders

When you go for custody orders, you'll be dealing with terms the law uses. Here's what they mean:

Petitioner is the person requesting orders. **Respondent** is the other person.

Joint physical custody means each parent will have significant periods of physical custody so the child will get frequent and continuing contact with both parents. It need not be 50/50; even 70/30 would be okay.

Joint legal custody means that both parents share the right and responsibility of making decisions related to the child's health, education and welfare.

Sole physical custody means the child will live with and be under the supervision of one parent. The other parent will usually get some form of visitation (see below). The terms, "primary physical custody" and "secondary physical custody" are often used instead—it has the same legal meaning but doesn't have the harsh implication that only one parent has the child. This allows the other parent to think of himself or herself as having less time rather than no custody.

Sole legal custody means that only one parent has the right and responsibility to make decisions related to the child's health, education, and welfare.

Mediation

Many judges want you to try conciliation (the court's term for mediation) before you bring a custody dispute to court. The way this works is different from county to county. The first time you go to a courtroom to get your papers signed by the judge, be *sure* to ask the clerk or judge if you are required to attend conciliation or mediation before the hearing. The possiblilities:

✦ you will be instructed to make a mediation appointment as soon as possible and try to complete mediation before the hearing.

✦ you will show up at the hearing and if Respondent is there, you will be asked to go immediately to see a mediator.

✦ you will not be required to mediate before the hearing.

If you are told you have to go through mediation or conciliation, ask for further instructions, then go home and read Appendix B.

3. Visitation orders

Specific times and places

It is important to set out visitation in detail in your application *and* in the proposed order. Always state when, where and how. If it isn't exactly clear, this leaves the whole matter open for interpretation, discussion, and more opportunities for contact and disagreement between you and the abuser. Look at the various orders we suggest in Chapter 15C for examples of visitation language. Also be sure to look at the parenting plan in Appendix B.

Restricting visitation

Visitation diary

Keep a written diary of all visits and cancelled visits for a period of time until the visitation plan is stabilized and peacefully in effect. This will give you a detailed record in case further action is required.

Monitored visitation.

If you believe that the children will be endangered by your partner if he is permitted to spend time alone with them, you can ask for monitored visitation. You must be able to explain and prove why the visits must be monitored. If you expect that this will be contested, get legal assistance. There are many variations on monitored visitation. One example is at Chapter 15C, Order 2: Monitored visitation, no contact, infant.

No contact—neutral pick-up and drop-off

If you want zero contact with your abuser, you can request an order for pick-up and drop-off of the child at a neutral, safe place, and keep your address and telephone number confidential. The place could be a friend or relative's house or a local police station. You can stay out of it by nominating a responsible neutral adult to transport the children. In extreme cases, the party returning the children to you should find a way to avoid being followed by Respondent so he can't find out where you are. An example of a neutral drop-off order is at Chapter 15C, Order 3: Neutral pick-up and drop-off.

No clothes and toys exchanged

If your court orders eliminate issues the parties might need to discuss, Respondent will have no excuse for contact. He can't "get at" Petitioner and a structured peace will prevail. For example, you could include terms in your order that Respondent keep his own separate set of clothes and toys for the child and that none will be exchanged. Likewise, include any other matters that you can determine ahead of time to remove any excuse for contact or discussion.

4. Child and spousal support

When you apply for a restraining order, you can also request orders for child support. In addition to child support, you can request that Respondent be ordered to maintain health insurance for you and the children, and that medical expenses for the children be paid by entirely by Respondent or shared. Medical expenses and health insurance are discussed below.

Remember, DVRO orders only last three years, so at some point you may want to get child support orders in a family law action that will last as long as the child is a minor.

No spousal support in a DVRO action

You can't get spousal support in a DVRO action. Go ahead and get your DVRO, but if you need spousal support, you should file a family law action for it as soon as possible. If you wait, you will weaken your chances for showing that you need support.

How much child support?

California has statewide guidelines for child support that the judge *must* follow. Because the formula is so complicated, most judges and lawyers use a computer program to do the calculating. Your financial details go in and the correct child support number comes out. The only issue is whether or not the financial data used was accurate and that issue can be settled simply by looking at pay stubs, tax returns and financial records.

The judge may or may not be willing to run your figures; it takes a little time. Many legal clinics and some paralegals have child support software. For $50, you can get your own excellent software called CalSupport. Look in your local bookstore for "How to Settle Child and Spousal Support," or order it by phone from Nolo Press at (800)464-5502. It's better than the $500 professional programs and is easy to use and understand.

Evidence of income

If you request child support, you will need documents to prove his income and you will want to bring these records to court with you. If you have no documents, you can try testifying as to what you know about his income, but the court may not be persuaded and you may not get a satisfactory support order.

There are various ways to prove income; for example, copies of pay stubs, bank records showing payroll deposits, tax returns, and business records. If you shared joint bank accounts, the bank will give you copies of your account records. Similarly, an accountant must give you copies of any documents you signed.

If you filed a joint tax return, the IRS will send a you a copy if you send in a written request. If he is employed, you can subpoena his payroll records as described in Appendix C. In either case, it will take some time, so get started immediately. If Respondent is self-employed and you did not file a joint return, hire a paralegal or an attorney to subpoena his bank records. This is a process similar to the subpoena of the payroll records; however, the subpoena of bank records is more complex and beyond the scope of this book.

Aid for Families with Dependent Children (AFDC)

If you are not employed, and he is not supporting you, you may want to apply for Aid for Families with Dependent Children (AFDC). This aid can be given immediately if you ask for immediate emergency aid. Contact your county welfare office or legal aid office to learn more about aid programs.

District Attorney child support action

You can ask the District Attorney's office to proceed against Respondent for child support. If Respondent is employed and able to pay a reasonable support, however, do not rely on the DA. Get your own support order. Many District Attorney's offices are overloaded, and they may take a very long time to deal with your case.

5. Health insurance, medical expenses, special needs

If you already have health insurance for yourself and your children on *his* policy, ask for an order that Respondent maintain you and the children on the policy. If he and the children are on *your* policy and you are paying an extra premium for this, ask for an order that he pay the premium for the children's and his health insurance or that he be removed.

If you are married, consider filing a family law action that will place an automatic restraint on all insurance policies, assets and liabilities.

If you have extraordinary medical or health related expenses for a child of you and the abuser, list these on the hardship section of the Income and Expense Declaration forms and also in your application. Explain these in your declaration and ask for whatever special orders you might need. For example,

"Our child is autistic and attends a special school five days a week. This program requires a co-payment of $500 a month. I need an order that Respondent pay one-half this expense in addition to child support. In addition, I need specially trained care when she is home with me. This costs about $400 a month. I need an order that Respondent pay one-half this expense in addition to child support."

Be sure these requests are included in your Orders. For an example of a special needs order, see Chapter 15C, Order 4: Special needs.

Be sure to list all special expenses in your documents. The court is not limited to the guideline child support amount where there are special needs.

6. What to do about your residence

Possession of the family home—the kick-out order

If you or your dependents are likely to suffer emotional or physical harm if Respondent is not excluded from the family home, you can request that he be ordered out. Courts are reluctant to issue such orders unless your showing of likely harm is strong and clear, so take special care with the preparation of your declaration and evidence.

To get this order, you have to show the following facts in your declaration:

✦ *You have the right to be there.* If you were living there prior to the filing, you probably have a right to stay. If you are on a month-to-month rental with no written agreement and the landlord knows you are living there just like Respondent is, you have a right to be there. If your name is on the title, lease or rental agreement, state this in your declaration and bring documents to the hearing if possible. However, if you are living with him in someone else's house, you cannot kick him out unless they kick him out for you.

✦ *Threat of harm.* You must be able to truthfully state under penalty of perjury facts showing that you or your dependents are likely to suffer emotional or physical harm if Respondent is not excluded.

✦ *He has someplace to go.* This isn't required legally, but it will help a lot if you can state in your declaration that he has someplace to go, or resources to pay for an apartment or hotel. For example, his parents live near his work and he can stay with them; or, he has complete facilities at his business and he can stay there; or, he can stay with his brother; or at a friend's house. All of these have been accepted by courts at one time or another. List one or two of his options in your declaration.

Kick-out without notice

If your abuser has hit you recently or has hit you in the past and you are under an *immediate* threat or fear of further violence, you can ask to have him removed *without notice to him.* This requires that your declaration show why it's not safe to give even short notice; for example: "I can't notify Respondent because if I do, he will steal the children and take them to Mexico. His parents have a home there and he will leave them there with his parents"; or, "I can't give Respondent notice because we have a history of verbal and physical abuse, and he has threatened to beat me if I try to do anything about it. Unless he is restrained without notice, I fear he will attack me."

Kick-out with notice

If there is no threat of immediate physical or emotional harm to you or the children, then you must call him the day before the hearing and let him know that you are going to court to get an order to have him removed from the home. You have to tell him the date, time and place of the hearing. In Los Angeles, for example, he must have at least six business hours notice, so you have to call no later than 11 am the day before the hearing. If you can't reach him, this will have to be explained and may affect your ability to get the order.

Risk assessment

Some people are afraid to apply for an order kicking him out because they are afraid that this will make him even more angry. Assess this risk with your counselor and support group. This is one of many important ways a good counselor and support group can help you.

Respondent may be permitted to return for clothing

Be prepared for the court to allow him a specified time to return to the house for his clothing and personal possessions. At the hearing, ask the court to name a day when you know you can have someone present. It can be an off-duty police officer or several friends. He may also be permitted to bring a support person. Videotape or photograph the house before, during and after his return with a support person present. Permit him to do the same. This may sound silly, but it helps to keep the peace. Make a special note of anything that may be important to you.

Practical security measures

✦ *Get some company.* Consider having someone stay with you for several weeks until the situation calms down. It helps to have the stabilizing influence of a support person during the first few weeks after he has notice of the restraining order proceedings.

✦   *Home security.* Change the locks, install security devices, get a guard dog, close the drapes at night, check the fences, gates, locks, alert the neighbors, change your phone number to an unlisted number, screen your calls with an answering machine.

If you let him move back in

If you permit him back into the house *before* the hearing and do not go to the hearing, the initial temporary restraining order expires. If you let him back in *after* the hearing and after an order has been issued, the order remains in effect; however, you have created a practical problem if the police are called. Get straight in your head what you are doing before you let him back in the house.

Ownership of the house

If you and your abuser own your home or are buying it, there may be property issues. No book can cover all the possible variations on this theme. If possible, hire an attorney for a consultation and get the advice you need before you file your action. This is better than getting halfway into it and finding out you have done something to damage your rights, or have forgotten to ask for something important.

House payments

For example, let's say you are employed but do not make enough to support yourself and the children and cover the house payments. You can request that the Respondent be ordered to make house payments, car payments or pay other bills in addition to child and spousal support. The court form provides for this request.

Tax issues

If you move out of a house that you own together, this may have a tax consequence. However, if you are absent temporarily for a short time there probably will be no tax consequence. A temporary departure to a shelter will not affect your tax situation. However, he may fight being removed from the home, claiming negative tax effects if he is removed. Too bad. He forfeited that option when he became violent. You might be able to agree that the house can remain his "permanent residence" for tax purposes until all property issues are resolved and for no other purpose. In other words, he can't reside there but he can use the address for tax purposes. This is a temporary, not a permanent solution. You will need further advice from a CPA versed in family law tax issues to cover the long-term tax effects of his removal from the home. In the domestic violence action, the court is more concerned with your personal safety. Focus on that.

Protecting against forgery

When you file for a DVRO you can ask the court to order him to make the mortgage payments and enjoin him from transferring or encumbering title to the house. Record a certified copy of the order and make sure the full street address and legal description are included in the order. If the property is held in joint tenancy and you are concerned that he may forge your name on a deed, speak to a qualified attorney about severing the Joint Tenancy. This will give you full and exclusive title to your half of the property. It will also cause both of you to lose the right of survivorship—the right of survivorship means that if you die, he owns 100% of the house and if he dies you own 100% of the house.

Foreclosure

If you are concerned that he will let the house go into foreclosure speak to an attorney. Consider contacting the bank and ask them to send notices regarding the mortgage to your post office box so you will be sure to know what is going on with the loan. You may be able to work out a temporary restructure of the loan and get the court to approve it if he does not cooperate. If there is little or no equity in the house and he stops payments, you may let the house go into foreclosure if you have no means to make the payments. If this happens, the foreclosure may take as long as six months to a year. The point is, you don't have to move immediately. Try to make a deal with the bank to restructure the payment plan or bring in a paying roommate. A rent-paying roommate who also serves as a "bodyguard" is another practical solution. Choose carefully, check references. You do not want to bring another problem into your home.

7. Bank Accounts

Right to funds

A big distinction must be made between married people and non-married people. If you are married, you are as much entitled to manage and control the community assets and funds as he is. You are entitled to at least one-half of the community funds in all accounts and you are entitled to exercise management and control over all the funds. If you have a joint account, there is no question about your access and right to the funds in that account.

If you are not married and you have joint accounts, the situation is different. If you have an agreement about ownership of the funds, then that controls. If you do not have an agreement, a judge may (or may not) trace where the money came from. In other words, if he is working and you are not, and it is only his income going into the joint account, it is his unless you have an agreement that it is also yours. You can't take the money unless you have a prior agreement or he somehow owes it to you.

Taking funds for support

Some wives take their fair share of the property and also take an amount for child or spousal support. This is risky. Technically, the court could order that these funds be returned. If, on the other hand, you leave a note and explain your thinking and if your partner is a practical person, he may understand after his initial reaction is over. If you need support and you want to avoid the initial legal expense of getting a support order, this practical solution can save both of you money. This "self-help" remedy is only practical if he is also left with enough cash to function.

8. Cars

If you have two cars and you each have one to drive, then you should preserve this situation by asking for an order that grants you the exclusive right to drive your car. If there is no marriage, the cars are his, and there are no children, the car will be given back to him unless he agrees otherwise. If there are children, the court may order him to permit you to use a car as part of a child support order. If you need him to pay for car payments and auto insurance, ask for this in your application, put it in the order, and explain why at the hearing.

If you own the car or are given the exclusive use of it and you are concerned that he may try to take it away from you or have it repossessed, change the door and ignition locks, park off the street, and do not keep any confidential papers or other valuables in the car.

9. Businesses

If you and your abuser own a business and you are running this business mostly on your own, ask for an order that you have exclusive possession of it and that you continue to run the business without interference and keep the income to support yourself and the children. Agree to keep records and make them available to him for inspection at reasonable times with reasonable notice. You will want the advice of an attorney to assist you with handling your business. Get advice before you take action. If you can safely do so, get copies of your business income and expense records and records of assets and debts. Take these with you to the attorney.

10. Guns

If he has threatened you with a gun, ask that he be ordered to remain at least 300 yards away from you and all restrained places—not just the normal 100 yards. The rationale? If bullets are involved, you need a greater distance. This is court policy in some districts and should be statewide law. Ask for it. If you want the guns sold or removed, ask for these orders. The court will order that he deposit weapons with the police for safekeeping during the time of the order and pay the storage on this. If you own weapons yourself, get rid of them. Don't set yourself up by having him break in and use them on you. It is quite common for the owner of a weapon to have it used against her. If you leave guns around the house with children present, it is not only dangerous, it is also a crime. Get rid of them.

Once a restraining order is issued, the law makes it a crime for the abuser to buy firearms during the term of the order.

11. Lost earnings and expenses

After notice and hearing, the court can order Respondent to repay you for expenses directly caused by his abuse—this is called restitution, and can include lost earnings, expenses for medical care, and the cost of temporary housing. Gather all medical and other bills and attach them to your declaration as exhibits or present them at the hearing. Restitution does *not* include an award for pain and suffering. You can get that if you sue him in a civil action.

12. Immigration issues

The basic rule is that it is not necessary to stay with an abuser to protect your immigration status. On the other hand, immigration laws are complex and change regularly, so it would be safest for you to take questions about your immigration status to an attorney who is an immigration law specialist.

Permanent residents (green card). If you are a permanent resident, you will not lose that status because you file for a restraining order. If you want to file for a divorce and have been married to a citizen for less than two years, your status will not be threatened if the divorce is caused by child or spousal abuse.

Conditional residents. If you hold a conditional resident status, and your application for permanent residence status depends on Respondent's cooperation, you can apply for the "battered spouse" waiver of the joint petition requirement. This means you can apply for permanent residence yourself, without help from your abusive husband. Divorce is not required, but it is easier to get the waiver if one is filed. You must show either that you would face extreme hardship if deported, or that the marriage was entered into in good faith but ended because of child or spouse abuse during the marriage. Good faith is shown by wedding photographs, joint checking accounts, and statements from friends. Your address is confidential and will not be disclosed to the abuser.

Undocumented aliens. Nothing in the DVRO procedure calls for checking documentation, so there should be no threat to an undocumented alien who needs a restraining order. If called to assist, police are not supposed to ask the victim for proof of citizenship or alien status. You are entitled to the same protection from violence, and the same court orders, regardless of your status. Most shelters do not check identification or documentation.

13. Interpreters

If you are not fluent in English, bring a friend with you to court who can serve as an interpreter. This person should be someone who understands domestic violence, and who will interpret accurately what is being said by all parties in the courtroom.

14. Attorney fees and court costs

In your application and proposed order, always check the box requesting that Respondent pay your attorney fees and costs. This is so you will be covered in case you later decide to hire an attorney. A judge has the power to order you to pay Respondent's attorney fees and court costs, but that would only happen in very rare cases where the judge becomes convinced that you falsely accused the Respondent with no basis in fact.

PART FOUR

HOW TO GET YOUR RESTRAINING ORDER

Chapter 12

Getting started

Can you do it yourself?

Yes! You *can* get your own restraining order. Thousands of Californians just like you do it themselves every year, so you can almost certainly do it too. Your chances of success go way up when you get involved with a support group, women's shelter and domestic violence counselor.

Yes! You *should* get your own restraining order, especially if the alternative is to remain a victim. You *can* do it.

DVRO or family law action—which is for you?

If you are married to the abuser or have a child with him, you have a choice to make; others can skip this section. You can get restraining orders either by filing a Domestic Violence Restraining Order (DVRO) or as part of a family law action, such as divorce, separation, annulment, paternity, and actions for child custody, visitation, and support. So which is best for you? Let's compare:

✦ **Speed.** You can get fast ex parte temporary orders in either action.

✦ **Ease.** The DVRO is easier to do, requires fewer forms to start.

✦ **Cost.** There is no filing fee for a DVRO. A family action requires a $182 filing fee unless you are very poor and eligible for a fee waiver.

✦ **Duration of orders.** DVRO orders expire after three years. Family law orders last indefinitely.

✦ **Spousal support orders** are not available under a DVRO.

No family actions pending

If you do not now have a family action pending, file for a DVRO first. It's cheaper and faster. But DVRO actions last only three years. If you are married to your attacker or have a child with him, you will want some orders that last much longer, so it is important that you go on to file a family action for permanent orders as soon as you get settled and stable.

Family action already pending

The law says that there should only be one action on the same subject between the same parties at the same time. If you already have a family action going, you can get restraining orders in that case. If you attempt to bypass the other case and file for a DVRO, there are several possible outcomes, depending on circumstances and the judge:

♦ some judges will refuse the DVRO and send you back to the other case, especially if the family action is in the same county.

♦ some judges will grant your DVRO anyway.

♦ some judges will grant emergency orders long enough to give you time to file for a restraining order in the other case or make motions to transfer and consolidate the cases.

How the issue is raised. If your family action is in the same county, the judge may already know about it. Otherwise, the Application, item (18), asks if you have another family action pending. Finally, the issue can be raised by Respondent if he wants to make an issue of it in court.

What to do? If you have a family action in the same county, you should file for restraining orders in that case. Otherwise, it is probably easier and faster for you to file for a DVRO first—that's what this book is about. If the judge expresses concern about your other family action, ask the judge for emergency orders to give you time to take legal action in the other jurisdiction. Ask for 120 days. Then get some legal advice about how best to proceed. This book does not cover getting orders in a family action, or transferring and consolidating cases.

Where your case can be filed

You can file in the county where you live or where the abuser lives. If there are branch courts in your county, your use of them is also determined by where either party lives. If you move to get away from the abuser, you can consider yourself a resident of your new location if you plan to stay there, or of the place you temporarily left if you plan to return. File in the location that is convenient to you.

Be sure to complete your case

Legal clinics report that many women don't realize that their temporary restraining orders expire in 21 days and do not return to court for the hearing. Their orders then lapse. Other women reconcile and just let the hearing date go. Don't do this. If you want to cancel the hearing, at least call the court and explain why. A better practice is to come to the hearing in person and explain the result of the first order. You may need to use this court again some day.

How to use the forms in this book

There is a complete set of forms in the back of this book—maybe more than you need—so just use the ones you need as explained in the instructions. Forms are also available at your county clerk's office for a fee, or you can order a complete set from Nolo Press. Send $6 to Nolo Press, P.O. Box 722, Occidental, CA 95465.

In the following chapters, you will find a description of each form with detailed instructions on how to fill it out. But first, here are some general instructions that apply to all the forms:

Petitioner, Respondent, in pro per

The Petitioner is you—the person who files papers, goes to court (if necessary), and gets things done. The Respondent is the abuser. In some forms, Petitioner is called "plaintiff" and Respondent is called "defendant." The words "in pro per" appear in the caption and at other places. This is legal Latin, meaning that you are appearing for yourself without an attorney. In some states, they use the term "pro se" which means the same thing.

Names

Although not required, it is a good idea to use full names. Where appropriate, you can add other names the abuser uses as secondary names; put AKA (also known as) before each. Be consistent: names should appear exactly the same way each time, including your signatures. The court will not know, for instance, that John Smith, J. W. Smith, John W. Smith and J. Wilson Smith are different names for the same person. It is better to type in the names in capitals. Use the names in normal order—last names go last. Use the wife's married name, unless the form asks specifically for her maiden name, or she used her maiden name during the marriage.

Your address and telephone number

If you don't want the abuser to know where you are, you can keep your home, office, and any other address or telephone number confidential. It is not necessary to put them on the forms. At the same time, the court needs to have an address and telephone number where you can be reached. This must be a reliable contact. Many people rent a post office box with a street address (you can't put a P.O. box on the court forms), and use a friend's phone number.

The Certificate of Assignment requires an address to prove to the court that the filing district is the proper district. This too can be marked "confidential," and the address left off.

General instructions

Get it together. Keep your papers safe, organized, and all together in one place.

Make copies. Before you fill them out, make some copies of the forms in the back of this book so you will always have a blank one in case you want to start over. If you are filling out one of these copies to use as an *original* for the court, make sure the back (if any) is copied upside down (tumbled) just as it appears in this book. Some courts will not accept originals that are not tumbled.

Type: Use a typewriter if at all possible, with larger size type (pica)—at least one county (San Diego) has refused forms with smaller type (elite). If you absolutely can't get a typewriter, use a *black* ballpoint pen and print very neatly.

Number of copies: The court gets the original of each form, Respondent gets a copy and you keep a copy for your files. So you need the original and two copies, but make at least one extra copy just in case. Some counties want an extra copy of each form when you file your papers in a branch office.

Doing it: Type each form carefully, check for errors, then make three copies. To find a copy machine nearby, check the yellow pages of your phone book under "copying and duplicating services," or look at a convenience mailbox service or a local library. When you make copies of a form that has material on the back, you will end up with two pages—staple them together at the top left-hand corner.

Recycled paper: All documents are to be filed on *recycled* paper so, when you make copies of forms in this book, use *recycled* paper. How clerks will check this is a mystery—probably they can't tell.

Color your world. Clerks have discovered colored paper and now some counties (Orange, San Diego, Sonoma) want some forms on colored paper. Humor them. Call your clerk and find out if they need colors. If they do, copy the blank forms in this book onto whatever color paper they want at your neighborhood copy shop.

Picky, picky. We've heard that Fresno won't accept forms directly from this book because they are ever-so-slightly less than 8½" × 11". Okay, make copies of the blank forms you need and you'll end up with full-sized paper.

Los Angeles bluebacks and other details: In Los Angeles County the court requires that each original document presented for filing be "bluebacked." This means that you get some sheets of 8½" × 14" blue heavyweight manuscript covers, then for each form, type the name of the form (as it appears at the bottom of the form) one-half inch from the bottom of the blue sheet on the right side. Fold the top two inches of the blue paper over the top of your document and staple it (and any attachments to that form) three times across the top. The blue paper and the typed label should now show one inch below the form. The package is now two-hole punched at the top. The clerks have punches and may be willing to help you with all this. Bluebacks are generally available at the clerk's form window or a stationery store. Filed forms must also be on recycled paper, tumbled (the back is upside down), and two-hole punched. Two-hole punches are available at the clerk's office and in the courtrooms.

Chapter 13

Checklist: A step-by-step guide

This is exactly what you do, step-by-step, to get your restraining order. Detailed instructions for each step are covered in the following chapters. Put a bookmark here so you can easily refer back to this list.

1. Call the Superior Court Clerk's office or go in to ask about local forms and procedures. Tell them you will be filing an application for a Domestic Violence Restraining Order. Ask them:

✦ Is there a branch court nearer to me than the main branch? *Write down the address and phone number of the court where you will be filing.*

✦ Are there printed local instructions for people filing DVRO cases?

✦ Where exactly do I go to file papers for a domestic violence restraining order? *Find out exactly how to get to the right room, desk or window.*

✦ Where is the courtroom where DVRO matters are heard? *Get the location, instructions for how to get to that courtroom and the phone number there.*

✦ Does the court hear live testimony from witnesses or consider only their declarations? *You may need to call the clerk in the courtroom for this one.*

✦ Are any local forms required in a DVRO case? *If so, go get them.*

    For filing in a branch court?

    For setting a hearing?

    For Ex Parte Declarations Re Notice?

    For anything else?

✦ Does the court have a domestic violence clinic? *If so, get the address and hours.*

✦ How much notice to Respondent is required in this county before an ex parte hearing (your first trip to the courtroom)?

✦ Are colored forms required for any part of a DVRO case?

✦ Do the originals of double-sided forms have to be filed "tumbled" (with the second page upside down on the reverse of the first page) or can you just submit two pages stapled together? If so, is this true for copies as well?

✦ Do forms have to be two-hole punched?

2. Fill out the forms. (Chapters 15–16):

✦ Application and Declaration for Order

✦ Order To Show Cause and Temporary Restraining Order

✦ Restraining Order After Hearing

✦ Declaration Re Ex Parte Notice

✦ Proof of Service

✦ *Local forms, if any, required by your county.* (For example, Los Angeles requires the DVRO–Law Enforcement Information form.)

✦ *If you have children with the abuser and want an order for child support, also file:* Income and Expense Declaration.

✦ *If your children are the subject of another custody action or court proceeding or have not lived with you or Respondent, also file:* Declaration Under Uniform Child Custody Jurisdiction Act (UCCJA).

3. Getting your case started (Chapter 17):

a. Give notice to the abuser. If you want immediate temporary orders, you must either notify the abuser the day before you file your papers, or explain in the Declaration Re Ex Parte Hearing why you can't give notice; for example, you fear Respondent will attack you if you give him notice.

b. File your forms, see the judge. Go to the clerk's office and file your forms. What you do next differs from court to court; the clerk will explain. Take your papers to the courtroom that handles DVRO matters. If you are asking for immediate temporary orders, wait to see the judge. The judge may ask a few questions, but it will be quite informal. This step is called the first hearing or the ex parte hearing.

c. If you have children with Respondent, ask the clerk or judge if you are required to go through conciliation or mediation before the hearing.

d. Get a hearing date. After the judge signs your papers, two dates will be set: the date for the hearing and the date by which Respondent must be served. You should ask for two days, but the court may require five days' notice before the hearing.

e. Get five certified copies of the Order from the clerk before you leave, and get the clerk's and bailiff's names and the courtroom phone number. You may need to call the department before the second hearing.

f. Custody mediation. If you have children with the abuser and there is a custody dispute, make an appointment with the conciliation office. They will notify Respondent. Remember, you are not required to attend any sessions with your abuser and you are permitted to have a support person with you at all sessions. Before you go, prepare a parenting plan. Work with your counselor or support group on this. Attend the sessions and present your plan.

g. Deliver a copy of the Order to each law enforcement agency near where you live and work (in L.A. County, hand them the DVRO–Law Enforcement form). Keep a copy of the Order with you at all times.

4. Serve the abuser. (Chapter 18).

a. Have Respondent personally served with the papers before the deadline date on the face of the Order to Show Cause. If served by a friend, prepare the Proof of Service form and make sure it is filled out correctly and signed by the person who served Respondent.

b. File the Proof of Service with the Clerk.

c. Deliver copies of the Proof of Service and the Order with the police departments where you live, work, and where the children go to school.

5. Prepare for the hearing (Chapter 19). Start this as soon as possible.

6. Go to the hearing (Chapter 20). Present your case.

7. After the hearing (Chapter 20).

    a. Paperwork. File your papers at the clerk's office and get five certified copies of the Order After Hearing.

    b. Deliver a copy of the Order to each law enforcement agency near where you live and work (in L.A. County, also hand them the DVRO–Law Enforcement form). Keep a copy of the Order with you at all times.

Make extra copies and make sure you keep one original certified copy.

    c. Other notice. Copies of the Order should be delivered to security officers (if any) at your work or residence and to the school administration if children are protected in the Orders. Ask friendly neighbors to be alert and call the police if they hear sounds of violence from your place.

    d. Wage Assignment Order. If this was issued, serve it on Respondent's employer by mail and file a Proof of Service by mail.

    e. Serve Respondent. If Respondent did not attend the hearing, he must be personally served with the order. Then file the Proof of Service with the Court clerk, and keep a "conformed" (stamped) copy of the Proof showing the date filed.

    f. Practical steps. Restraining orders are very effective but don't make you bulletproof. Continue to take all practical steps to protect yourself. Stay out of Respondent's orbit. Granted, you may be "entitled" to go certain places, but life will be much more peaceful if you stay away from him and the places you know he will be. Follow through with any criminal action filed by the city or district attorney's office. If you have lost wages for days you attend hearings, or any other damages which you cannot collect from Respondent, consider filing a claim with the Crime Victim's Assistance Fund. Your local police department or legal aid office will have information about this.

Chapter 14

How to make your case—statements in the forms

The presentation you make at your hearing is directly related to the statements you make now in your Application. If you can, review Chapter 19 *before* you fill out the Application so you understand how a case is made and presented in court. As soon as possible after your case is filed, get Respondent served and start preparing for your hearing.

Concise vs. complete

Your statements need to be very concise—directly to the point and in as few words as possible—but also complete. If you are requesting "extraordinary" relief—orders that are very intrusive on Respondent—your statements should be more detailed and, if possible, you should also include declarations from other witnesses to back up your story. For example:

✦ **Kick-out.** If you want Respondent ordered out of the house, you have to show that you have a right to be there and that harm to you or the children is a real possibility if he is allowed to remain. It will help if you also show that he has somewhere to go. See Chapter 11-6.

✦ **Supervised visitation.** This is a huge intrusion on Respondent's rights as a parent and will not be granted without very clear and convincing evidence showing that the children are likely to be abused, neglected or kidnapped unless visits are supervised. Statements of other witnesses will help here.

If your court does not hear testimony

Some courts do not take live testimony from witnesses in a DVRO action, but consider only the declarations on file. This means that your declarations and documents carry the whole burden of making your case. If this is the practice in your court, take extra care to make your statements complete and consider adding additional declarations from other witnesses (Chapter 16E). Make sure you have included every basic fact that is relevant and important.

It is important to find out if your court follows this rule before you complete the Application—or as soon as possible after it is filed—so you can consider adding additional declarations.

Tell the strict truth

Be accurate: don't minimize the facts and don't exaggerate. Make sure your statements are consistent with statements you made to police or other people. If the judge gets the idea that you are exaggerating, your case will be weakened and she might discount everything you say. If your case folds due to false or misleading statements, the judge could award attorney fees to Respondent. On the other hand, if you minimize the facts, you may not get the orders you need. Tell it straight.

Respondent will read your statements when he is served with papers before the hearing. Experience shows that Respondents are more likely to fight the case if some part of the story is exaggerated or false. On the other hand, they eventually accept the "new reality" more quickly if you tell the story exactly the way it happened, because they ultimately respect the truth. An improved future relationship is important if you have children together.

Guide for writing statements

Give dates (or approximate dates) whenever possible. Refer to yourself as "I" and the abuser as "Respondent." Don't waste space with irrelevant facts, opinions or general conclusions. Don't tell why he hit you or what you were arguing about or what a bad temper he has. Here's an example of how *not* to do it:

> Respondent's whole family is full of alcoholics. He's had an alcohol problem since he was fourteen and gets so frustrated from it that he can't control his anger and this causes him to get violent and hit me. On 1/25/96, we were arguing about his drinking and he hit me so bad I got sick to my stomach and had to go to the hospital.

Stick to bare, essential facts. Give dates, times, places and tell very briefly what happened. Here's how to do the previous statement correctly:

> On 1/25/96, at about 5:30 pm, Respondent came home and hit and kicked me. I was so hurt that I had to go to a hospital to be treated for bruises and cuts. I was on out-patient for two weeks.

Here is how to go about writing your statement. Assume the Application was filed in late January, 1996:

1. Describe the most recent event.

On 1/25/96, at about 10 pm at our home, Respondent hit me in the face. I tried to run away, but he grabbed me and threw me against the wall.

If you were not hit but are afraid, explain what he did to cause you to be afraid:

On 1/25/96, at about 10 pm at the apartment we share, Respondent threatened to kill me. He showed me a gun and said he would use it on me unless I signed my car over to him.

If the most recent event was not very recent, explain why you are filing now:

Respondent has been out of the state since he hit me on 9/17/95. I just learned that he is coming back on 1/29/96, and he told me when he left he would "take care" of me when he gets back. I am afraid he will attack me and need the order now.

2. Describe how the event ended.

He left for work and told me I had until 10 am the next day to sign the papers.

3. If you have children, state if they were present.

Our 4-year-old girl was in the same room with us the whole time, crying hysterically.

4. If he owns or has threatened you with weapons, say so.

Respondent owns several guns and combat knives. He has threatened to use them on me on numerous occasions, including 10/30/95, 12/22/95 and 1/25/96.

5. Describe the next two most recent events if there were any.

6. Describe the general pattern or background, briefly.

Respondent became verbally abusive about two years ago. About nine months ago he began to shove me. It's getting worse. He has hit me, pulled my hair, and shoved me around about once a week for the last six months. He often does it in front of the children. He used to say he was sorry, but not for a long time. He isn't sorry any more.

7. Police and medical reports.

If you called the police, or if you received medical treatment or went to a therapist, or had to repair damage done by Respondent, state what happened and attach copies of police reports, medical reports and bills from doctors, therapists or repairmen. Do it like this:

> The police came out on 1/25/96 at about 11:45 am and took a report, I then went to the hospital. Copies of the police report, hospital report and medical bill are attached.

8. Witnesses.

If you are asking for extraordinary relief (kick-out orders, supervised visitation) it will help if you have a witness to back up your statements. A relative is good; an independent witness is even better. Get the witness to make a statement on the Declaration form (Chapter 16E). Refer to the witness's statement and attach copies to your Application, like this:

> The events of 1/25/96 were observed by my neighbor, Jane Doe. Her declaration is attached.

Chapter 15

Forms required in every case

Need extra space? It would be nice if your statements and orders fit in the spaces provided in the forms. If not, no problem—attach an Additional Page (Chapter 16A).

A. Application and Declaration for Order

Complete this form in every case—it *is* your case. It gives the court details about the person or persons to be protected, the person to be restrained, the bad conduct alleged and what orders you need to stop further abuse. There are two sheets, front and back, or four pages to fill out. Fill it out as shown in the illustrations and as described in the instructions below.

This is the longest form and takes the most care and thought to fill out. Once you've done this, the rest is downhill, relatively speaking.

In the instructions below, numbered text notes refer to the item numbers on the form. Letters are used for items that have no item number; these letters can be found on the illustrations of the forms.

15A-1: The Application and Declaration (page 1 of 4)

Caption. Items A–H on the illustration are collectively called the caption.

(A) **Your name.** First, middle, then last name. If you are also known by any other name(s), put it (them) here after AKA (also known as).

(B) **Your address.** If you don't want Respondent to know where you are, use a friend's or relative's address (one that he already knows), your work address if he already knows it, or go rent a PO Box. Respondent is going to get a copy of all forms, so be careful what information you disclose.

(C) **Your phone number.** Same options as address, except if you don't have a number you can safely disclose, type "None."

Fig. 15A-1: The Application and Declaration (page 1 of 4)

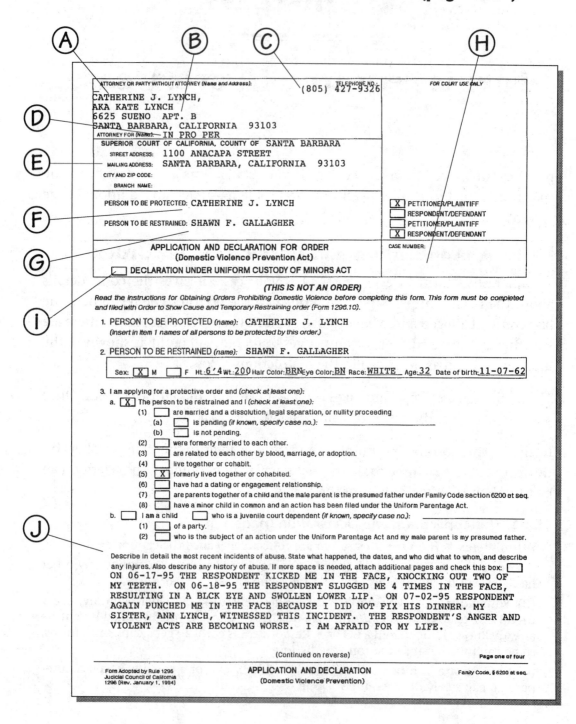

Ⓐ ATTORNEY OR PARTY WITHOUT ATTORNEY *(Name and Address)*:   (805) 427-9326   TELEPHONE NO.:   FOR COURT USE ONLY

CATHERINE J. LYNCH,
AKA KATE LYNCH
6625 SUENO APT. B
SANTA BARBARA, CALIFORNIA 93103
ATTORNEY FOR *(Name)*: IN PRO PER

SUPERIOR COURT OF CALIFORNIA, COUNTY OF SANTA BARBARA
STREET ADDRESS: 1100 ANACAPA STREET
MAILING ADDRESS: SANTA BARBARA, CALIFORNIA 93103
CITY AND ZIP CODE:
BRANCH NAME:

PERSON TO BE PROTECTED: CATHERINE J. LYNCH

PERSON TO BE RESTRAINED: SHAWN F. GALLAGHER

APPLICATION AND DECLARATION FOR ORDER (Domestic Violence Prevention Act) ☐ DECLARATION UNDER UNIFORM CUSTODY OF MINORS ACT	[X] PETITIONER/PLAINTIFF ☐ RESPONDENT/DEFENDANT ☐ PETITIONER/PLAINTIFF [X] RESPONDENT/DEFENDANT CASE NUMBER:

(THIS IS NOT AN ORDER)

Read the Instructions for Obtaining Orders Prohibiting Domestic Violence before completing this form. This form must be completed and filed with Order to Show Cause and Temporary Restraining order (Form 1296.10).

1. PERSON TO BE PROTECTED *(name)*: CATHERINE J. LYNCH
(Insert in Item 1 names of all persons to be protected by this order.)

2. PERSON TO BE RESTRAINED *(name)*: SHAWN F. GALLAGHER

Sex: [X] M ☐ F Ht: 6'4 Wt: 200 Hair Color: BRN Eye Color: BN Race: WHITE Age: 32 Date of birth: 11-07-62

3. I am applying for a protective order and *(check at least one)*:
   a. [X] The person to be restrained and I *(check at least one)*:
     (1) ☐ are married and a dissolution, legal separation, or nullity proceeding
       (a) ☐ is pending *(if known, specify case no.)*: _____
       (b) ☐ is not pending.
     (2) ☐ were formerly married to each other.
     (3) ☐ are related to each other by blood, marriage, or adoption.
     (4) ☐ live together or cohabit.
     (5) [X] formerly lived together or cohabited.
     (6) ☐ have had a dating or engagement relationship.
     (7) ☐ are parents together of a child and the male parent is the presumed father under Family Code section 6200 et seq.
     (8) ☐ have a minor child in common and an action has been filed under the Uniform Parentage Act.
   b. ☐ I am a child ☐ who is a juvenile court dependent *(if known, specify case no.)*: _____
     (1) ☐ of a party.
     (2) ☐ who is the subject of an action under the Uniform Parentage Act and my male parent is my presumed father.

Describe in detail the most recent incidents of abuse. State what happened, the dates, and who did what to whom, and describe any injuries. Also describe any history of abuse. If more space is needed, attach additional pages and check this box: ☐
ON 06-17-95 THE RESPONDENT KICKED ME IN THE FACE, KNOCKING OUT TWO OF MY TEETH. ON 06-18-95 THE RESPONDENT SLUGGED ME 4 TIMES IN THE FACE, RESULTING IN A BLCK EYE AND SWOLLEN LOWER LIP. ON 07-02-95 RESPONDENT AGAIN PUNCHED ME IN THE FACE BECAUSE I DID NOT FIX HIS DINNER. MY SISTER, ANN LYNCH, WITNESSED THIS INCIDENT. THE RESPONDENT'S ANGER AND VIOLENT ACTS ARE BECOMING WORSE. I AM AFRAID FOR MY LIFE.

(Continued on reverse)   **Page one of four**

Form Adopted by Rule 1296
Judicial Council of California
1296 (Rev. January 1, 1994)

APPLICATION AND DECLARATION
(Domestic Violence Prevention)

Family Code, § 6200 et seq.

(D) Type in "In Pro Per." This tells the world you are representing yourself.

(E) Court's name and addresses. Type in the county name in the court's title and enter the court's street address. If they have a P.O. box, enter that too.

(F) Your full name, exactly as in (A). If you want protection for any other members of your household, also enter their full names here. In the boxes to the right of the name, check the box for Petitioner/Plaintiff.

(G) The abuser's name. If his name is Robert, but he goes by Bobby, enter both names using AKA. For example, "Robert Brown, AKA Bobby Brown." In the boxes to the right of the name, check the box for Respondent/Defendant.

(H) Case number. Leave this blank. When you file your papers, the clerk will stamp in a case number. From now on, use this number on every document.

(I) UCCJA Declaration. Check this box if you also file the UCCJA Declaration (see item 5 below and Chapter 16B).

(1) Who is to be protected. Put your name exactly as entered in (A) and the names of anyone else in your family or household who needs to be protected. For children, include a birthdate. If Respondent is not the biological or legal father of the child, indicate it like this, "Brent Lynch, Petitioner's son, 8/5/88." Children you share with Respondent are not listed unless Respondent has actually abused the child in some way.

(2) Respondent's name and description. Enter his name exactly as entered at item (F). Fill in the physical description info as best you can to help police identify the abuser, but if you don't know an item, leave it blank. The clerk will probably give you another form also requesting information about Respondent, including his Social Security number and driver's license number. Give all information you can, but don't worry if you don't have everything requested; it will not affect whether or not you get the restraining orders.

(3)(a) Your relationship to Respondent. Check box (a) and any of the following boxes (1-8) that apply to your situation.

Item (2), "formerly married," means your divorce is final. Item (3) includes aunts, uncles, grandparents, in-laws, adopted children—it is a very loose definition of family. Items (4) or (5) apply if you and Respondent have regularly resided in the same place, as ordinary roommates or lovers, now or long ago.

Item (6) applies if you had even a single date with Respondent. However, in some cases you may not want to say this even if true. If some guy is obsessed with you, indicating that you have a "dating" relationship may encourage his unrealistic notion that you and he are "dating." A women's shelter or domestic violence counselor may be able to help you think this one out. If you decide it would be a mistake to indicate that a "dating" relationship exists, you can still obtain a Civil Harassment Restraining Order, although that is not covered in this book.

Item (7) should **not** be checked if you are trying to deny that Respondent has any rights to your children. Item (8) applies if Respondent denies being the father of your child and you have filed a Complaint to Establish Paternity.

(3)(b). Not for you. Don't check these boxes.

(J) Description of abuse. This states your case. It's the most important part of your application, so we're going to give it extra attention. *You* should, too. Your statements must clearly show that you are a victim of domestic abuse and that you need orders to protect you. If you want temporary restraining orders, you must show that you need the protection immediately, before there is a full hearing and with little or no notice to the abuser. Do it like this:

First, describe the most recent threat or incident. What caused you to file this application?

> Last night, on 6/7/95, Respondent grabbed me by the hair, hit me in the face four times and screamed that he could kill me anytime he felt like it. I had a black eye and bruises. I am terrified that he will attack again at any moment.

Next, describe recent incidents of abuse. What makes you believe the threat is real? What has been your history with him?

> On 5/3/95, he threw a toaster at me. On 3/3/95, I had to get emergency treatment for cuts received when he threw a dish at me. My sister saw this happen. Five times in the last three months he has struck me in the face and body.

c. State if children have been present at any incidents:

> He frequently yells at me and hits me in the presence of the children.

d. If Respondent owns weapons, say so and include threats to use them:

> Respondent owns a gun and has threatened to shoot me with it several times.

e. Mention special facts that are directly relevant to the threat of harm:

> Respondent has been diagnosed as bipolar manic depressive. He refuses to take his medication and often goes into rages when he is without it.

f. End with your fear of harm or emotional upset:

> I am constantly afraid of Respondent and believe that if not restrained he will continue to harass and harm me.

Be sure to include threats, injuries, medical treatments, and if he owns or has used or threatened to use weapons. Name anyone who was present at an incident.

If you need special orders, state exactly what you need and why.

> Respondent and I have been separated for two weeks. I have been living in a women's shelter and the children are in a new school. He does not know where we are. I attach the declarations of two friends who were present when he threatened to steal the children and take them to Mexico, and who can attest that he is ready, willing and able to take them. I need an order that the school remain confidential and that he have visitation only if monitored by an off-duty police officer selected by myself and paid by Respondent in advance of each visit. I need an order that he post a $50,000 bond payable to me if he does unlawfully remove the children. I need these funds to pay legal fees, travel expenses, and the costs to hire detectives to locate the children and enforce this order in Mexico.

Need more space? If your statement will not fit in the space on the form, check the box to indicate an Additional Page, type "See Attachment" on the form, and use the Additional Page (Chapter 16A) to make your statement.

Figure 15A-2: The Application and Declaration (page 2 of 4)

Ⓐ   Ⓑ

PERSON TO BE PROTECTED *(Name)*: CATHERINE J. LYNCH

PERSON TO BE RESTRAINED *(Name)*: SHAWN F. GALLAGHER

CASE NUMBER:
323404

(THIS IS NOT AN ORDER)

4. The person to be restrained has intentionally or recklessly *(check at least one)*:
   a. [X] caused or attempted bodily injury to me or another.
   b. [ ] caused or attempted sexual assault on me or another.
   c. [X] made me afraid of physical or emotional harm.
   d. [ ] made a family or household member *(names)*:   afraid of physical or emotional harm.

5. The person to be restrained and I *(you must check a or b)*:
   a. [ ] have no minor children.
   b. [X] have children [ ] who are juvenile court dependents *(if known, specify case no's.)*: _____

   Child's name   Birthdate
   RALPH L. GALLAGHER   12-17-90

   c. If you are seeking an order regarding custody or visitation of your minor children, complete the following:
      (1) Each child is now living with
          [X] me [ ] person to be restrained at *(address optional)*:

      (2) [X] Each child has lived only with me or the person to be restrained or both during the last five years.
      (3) [X] I have not participated in any litigation or proceeding in any state concerning custody of this child.
      (4) [X] I have no information about any pending custody proceeding or any person not a party to this proceeding who has physical custody or visitation rights concerning this minor child.
      (5) If you have **not** checked a box in each of items (1) through (4), you must attach a completed Declaration Under Uniform Custody of Minors Act *(Form no. MC-150)* and check this box: [ ] and the box at the top of the first page.

I REQUEST THE COURT TO MAKE THE ORDERS INDICATED BY THE CHECK MARKS IN THE BOXES BELOW.

⑥ₐ
⑥ᵦ
⑥꜀

6. [X] **RESTRAINING ORDERS**   [X] To be ordered now and effective until the hearing.
   Restrained person must not contact, molest, attack, strike, threaten, sexually assault, batter, telephone, or otherwise disturb my peace [ ] and that of the following family or household members *(names)*:

7. [X] **RESIDENCE EXCLUSION AND RELATED ORDERS**   [X] To be ordered now and effective until the hearing.
   Restrained person must immediately move from and must not return to *(address)*: 6625 SUENO APT. B
   SANTA BARBARA, CALIFORNIA
   and may take only personal clothing and effects.
   I have a legal right to live at the address above because *(specify facts and attach any document that supports your claim)*:
   I LIVED AT THE RESIDENCE FOR A YEAR, CONTRIBUTING TO THE RENTAL
   PAYMENT. I HAVE NOWHERE ELSE TO GO AND HAVE NO MONEY.

8. [X] **STAY-AWAY ORDERS**   [X] To be ordered now and effective until the hearing.
   Restrained person, who resides at *(state address if known)*:
   and works at *(state address if known)*:
   must stay at least *(specify)*: 100   yards away from the following persons and places *(the addresses of the places are optional and you do not have to reveal them)*:
   a. Myself
      [X] and the following family or household members *(names)*:

   b. [X] My residence *(address optional)*: 6625 SUENO APT. B SANTA BARBARA, CA

   c. [X] My place of work *(address optional)*:

   d. [X] The children's school or place of child care *(address optional)*:

   e. [X] Other *(specify)*: MY SISTER, ANN LYNCH'S HOUSE:
      (address optional): 6592 SABADO TARDE   SANTA BARBARA, CA

(Continued on next page)   Page two of four

1296 [Rev. January 1, 1994]

APPLICATION AND DECLARATION
(Domestic Violence Prevention)

Family Code, § 6200 et seq.

Figure 15A-2: The Application and Declaration (page 2 of 4)

(A) Short caption. Type in the names of the parties, exactly as entered in the caption on page 1, but omit aliases (AKA), if any.

(B) Case number. Leave it blank; the clerk will stamp your case number when you file your forms.

(4) Bad acts. Check boxes to indicate things Respondent has done. At (4)(d) list anyone in your family or household who Respondent has abused or threatened and who you want included in these restraining orders.

(5) Children. You *must* check a box to indicate whether or not you have minor children with Respondent. If your children are from another relationship, check (5)(a). If Respondent is the father of your children, check (5)(b) and list each child's name and birthdate. Check the second box at (5)(b) to indicate if any of the listed children are juvenile court dependents.

(5)(c) Custody and visitation. If you want orders for custody and visitation, complete items (5)(c)(1–4). Check each box if the statement is true. If any of those statements is not true, you *must* check box (5)(c)(5) and also attach a completed UCCJA Declaration (Chapter 16B). If you are required to complete the UCCJA Declaration, go to item (I) above and check the box.

Restraining orders

(6)(a) Basic restraining order. Check this box in every case. If you will need to talk to Respondent from time to time about the children, cross out the words "contact" and "telephone" in the sentence that follows.

(b) To be ordered now. Check this box if you want the order to go into effect immediately. If you do not check this box, you will not get restraining orders until the date of the hearing.

To grant these orders, the judge must be convinced that an emergency exists that justifies bypassing the legal requirement that both sides to a dispute have an opportunity to tell his or her side of the story. Your declarations in item 3 above must state facts that show you are in *immediate* danger of physical harm or emotional upset and that the abuse may continue without immediate court action.

(c) Protect others. If other family or household members are to be protected, check box (6)(b) and enter their names.

(7) Kick-out order. If you want Respondent ordered out of the family residence, check this box and enter the address of the residence. Do not check this box unless you have a legal right to be in the house or apartment (see Chapter 11-6).

To be ordered now. Check this box if you want the residence exclusion to go into effect immediately. If not checked, Respondent cannot be ordered out until the hearing date.

Declaration. State why you have a right to remain in the residence (see Chapter 11-6). State if you have nowhere else to go or have no money to go anywhere else and state whether Respondent is able to go somewhere else if he is forced out.

I have lived in the residence for a year and am named on the rental agreement. I have no money and nowhere to go. Respondent can live with his brother.

(8) Stay-away order. Check this box if you want Respondent to stay completely away from you. Enter Respondent's home address and work address or type in "unknown" for each one. Type in the specific number of yards Respondent is to stay away from you—this is typically 100 yards; 300 yards if he has a gun.

> **To be ordered now:** Check this box if you want the orders to take place immediately and stay in effect until the hearing.

> **(a)** Check this box and name any other persons to be protected.

> **(b)** Check this box if you want Respondent to stay away from your residence. You do not need to provide an address.

> **(c)** Check this box if you want Respondent to stay away from your workplace. You do not need to provide an address.

> **(d)** Check this box if you want Respondent to stay away from your children's school or child care facility. Make sure you give the school a copy of the restraining order when it is issued.

> **(e)** Check this box to keep Respondent away from any other place not already listed, such as your church, car or a friend's house.

Figure 15A-3: The Application and Declaration (page 3 of 4)

(A) Short caption. Type in the names of the parties, exactly as entered in the caption on page 1, but omit aliases (AKA), if any.

(B) Case number. Leave it blank; the clerk will stamp your case number when you file your forms.

(9) Custody and visitation. Check this box if you have children and want orders for custody and visitation. If you do not have children in common with Respondent, skip to item (11).

> **To be ordered now:** Check this box if you want the orders to take place immediately and stay in effect until the hearing.

> **(a) Custody.** Check this box if you want a custody order. Enter the full name of each child in the first column.

In the second column, write in your name if you would like sole physical custody of the child. If you want to share physical custody with Respondent, write in "Joint." For an explanation of custody terms, see Chapter 11-2. Joint physical custody implies a high degree of contact between the parents, so you will probably choose to have sole custody for one parent or the other. If you are staying in a shelter, you should put your name in both the second and third column, as shelters generally do not allow contact between you and Respondent.

In the third column, write in your name if you would like sole legal custody of the child. If you want to share legal custody with Respondent, write in "Joint." Joint

Figure 15A-3: The Application and Declaration (page 3 of 4)

(A)   (B)

PERSON TO BE PROTECTED *(Name)*: CATHERINE J. LYNCH	CASE NUMBER: 323404
PERSON TO BE RESTRAINED *(Name)*: SHAWN F. GALLAGHER	

(THIS IS NOT AN ORDER)

9. [X] **CHILD CUSTODY AND VISITATION**   [X] **To be ordered now and effective until the hearing.**

    a. [X] Custody *(see Instructions for Obtaining Orders Prohibiting Domestic Violence for an explanation of physical, legal, sole and joint custody)*

    I request the custody orders shown in the following columns:

List the child's name below	List the name of the parent who should get sole physical custody of the child below *(if you want physical custody to be joint, write the word "joint")*	List the name of the parent who should get sole legal custody of the child below *(if you want legal custody to be joint, write the word "joint")*
RALPH L. GALLAGHER	CATHERINE J. LYNCH	CATHERINE J. LYNCH

    b. [X] Visitation
    Restrained person should have the right to visit the children as follows:
    (1) [ ] None.
    (2) [ ] Supervised visitation.
    (3) [X] Visitation with the following other restrictions *(specify)*: VISITATION SHALL BE EVERY SUNDAY AT 1 P.M. TO MONDAY AT 5 P.M.   THE CHILD SHALL BE PICKED-UP AND DROPPED-OFF AT THE SANTA BARBARA POLICE DEPARTMENT, LOCATED AT 303 CABRILLO STREET, SANTA BARBARA, CA.

    c. I need this custody and visitation order because of the following facts *(specify)*: THE RESPONDENT IS SO VIOLENT THAT I AM AFRAID OF ANY CONTACT WITH HIM.   I AM ALSO FRIGHTEDED TO LEAVE HIM ALONE WITH RALPH FOR ANY LONGER PERIOD OF TIME.   THE RESPONDENT HAS A SEVERE DRINKING PROBLEM.

[If you request an order for child support, attorney fees, or costs, attach a completed Income and Expense Declaration (Form no. 1285.50).]

10. [X] **CHILD SUPPORT**
    a. [ ] I am receiving public assistance.
    b. [X] Restrained person should be ordered to pay support as specified, commencing on *(date)*: HEARING DATE

Child's name	Birthdate	Monthly amount
RALPH L. GALLAGHER	12-17-90	STATE GUIDELINES

    c. [ ] I request that a wage assignment be issued.

11. [X] **PROPERTY CONTROL**   [X] **To be ordered now and effective until the hearing.**
    a. I request that I be given the exclusive temporary use, possession, and control of the following property we own or are buying *(specify)*: RED VOLKSWAGON CONVERTIBLE, LIC #1E2U021   (1976)

    b. The order is necessary because *(specify)*: I NEED THE CAR TO GET TO WORK AND SCHOOL. THE RESPONDENT HAS A MOTORCYCLE HE CAN USE TO GET TO WORK.

(Continued on reverse)   Page three of four

1296 [Rev. January 1, 1994]   **APPLICATION AND DECLARATION**
(Domestic Violence Prevention)

legal custody need not involve a high degree of contact, so it may be less threatening if you give Respondent joint legal custody, and will certainly feel better to him.

In making a custody order, the judge considers what is in the best interests of the child, so will probably inquire into who has been primarily responsible for the child's care in the recent past, and whether or not there has been any child abuse.

(b) Visitation. When one parent is given physical custody the other usually gets visitation. The law encourages contact between the child and both parents, even if it has to be supervised.

(1) No visitation. Check this box if you can show that any amount of visitation would be dangerous or harmful to the child—for example, child abuse. State facts justifying this extreme measure at (9)(c); for example: "Respondent has threatened to take the children to his family home in Nigeria and never let me see them again."

(2) Supervised visitation. Check this box if you want Respondent to see the children only when supervised or monitored by a third party. State facts justifying this extreme measure at (9)(c); for example: "The children are endangered by Respondent's drinking and drunk driving, and terrified of Respondent's mood changes, and would not be secure being alone with him."

(3) Terms of visitation. If you want Respondent to have unsupervised visitation, check this box and type in a specific visitation schedule that is as specific as possible. For example, "Visitation shall be every Friday 6 pm to Sunday 1 pm. The children shall be picked up and dropped off at the Santa Barbara Police station, 303 Cabrillo St., Santa Barbara, CA." *Never* request "reasonable visitation."

If you can't decide how to handle visitation, just type in "To be determined in mediation."

Before the hearing, you will be required to go to a mediation session. In domestic violence cases, you can request separate sessions or you can mediate together and take a support person with you.

(c) Declarations. State facts showing that the orders you request are in the "best interests" of the child. If you want supervised visits, you need a strong, clear showing that children are likely to be harmed or stolen if visits are *not* supervised.

(10) Child support. Check this box if you want Respondent ordered to pay child support. Support cannot be ordered immediately, but only after the hearing—after Respondent has had notice and a chance to appear.

When you request child support, you also have to file the Income and Expense forms (Chapter 16C) and the Wage Assignment form. If you are in a big hurry for restraining orders and don't want to take the time to fill out those forms, just don't ask for child support now. You can come back to court for it later.

(a) If you are receiving welfare—AFDC, food stamps, etc.—check this box. The district attorney's office will be notified and will (some day) attempt to collect support from Respondent. It is their job to make sure able parents pay for their own children.

(b) Check this box if you are asking for support. Enter each child's full name in the first column and his or her birthdate in the second column. In the third column, under "monthly amount," write in "To be determined at hearing according to state guidelines."

(c) Check this box if you are requesting support. A wage assignment requires Respondent's employer to withhold money for support directly from his paycheck. Even if he is unemployed or self-employed, this order might be used in the future.

(11) Property control. Check this box if you want an order giving you the exclusive use of certain property that is jointly owned by you and Respondent—car, computer, TV, tools, whatever.

To be ordered now: Check this box if you want the orders to take place immediately and stay in effect until the hearing.

(a) List the property in detail: " White 1982 Mustang, Lic. #UTO673."

(b) Declaration. State why it is necessary that you have the exclusive use of the listed property. For example: "I need the car to take the children to day care and get to work; he doesn't work. I need the computer for my school work and he doesn't use it except for games."

Figure 15A-4: The Application and Declaration (page 4 of 4)

(A) Short caption. Type in the names of the parties, exactly as entered in the caption on page 1, but omit aliases (AKA), if any.

(B) Case number. Leave it blank; the clerk will stamp your case number when you file your forms.

(12) Attorney fees and costs. Check this box if you want Respondent to pay for attorney's fees, court and transportation costs related to this action. If you check this box, you will have to file completed Income and Expense Declaration forms. Because you may later decide to hire an attorney, it's a good idea to check this box. If you are asking for child support, you have to do the I and E forms anyway, so you might as well ask for attorney fees and costs, too.

(13) Restitution. Check this box if you want Respondent ordered to reimburse you for losing work or other expenses (other than legal costs, item 12) that were a direct result of Respondent's abuse. This can include damage to property, medical bills, the cost of new locks or of moving to a new home. This can't be ordered immediately, but will be considered at your hearing. You must be prepared to prove your expenses so gather up bills and receipts or other documents that support your claims.

(14) Counseling. Check this box only if you really want some type of counseling for Respondent. You do not have to attend together.

(a) Check this box if you want Respondent ordered into a batterers' treatment program.

(b) Check this box if you intend to continue living with Respondent and you want both of you to participate in separate counseling.

(c) Check this box if you want Respondent to pay for the costs of counseling.

Figure 15A-4: The Application and Declaration (page 4 of 4)

Ⓐ   Ⓑ

PERSON TO BE PROTECTED *(Name)*:	CATHERINE J. LYNCH	CASE NUMBER
PERSON TO BE RESTRAINED *(Name)*:	SHAWN F. GALLAGHER	323404

(THIS IS NOT AN ORDER)

12. ☐ **ATTORNEY FEES AND COSTS**
Restrained person should be ordered to pay attorney fees and costs as follows:

13. ☐ **RESTITUTION**
I request that restrained person should be ordered to pay the following lost earnings and other actual expenses or cost of services caused directly by the violence complained of:

Type of loss	Pay to	Amount of claim
		$

14. ☒ **COUNSELING**
   a. ☒ I request that restrained person be ordered to participate in batterer's treatment counseling.
   b. ☐ I will continue to live with restrained person and I request that we both be ordered to participate in counseling at separate times and places ☐ and that restrained person, who is able to do so, be ordered to pay the costs of the counseling.

15. ☒ **OTHER ORDERS** *(specify other orders you request to help carry out the orders previously requested)*:
   1.   THAT THE RESPONDENT BE ORDERED TO MAINTAIN ANY HEALTH CARE INSURANCE HE HAS FOR RALPH AND MYSELF.
   2.   THAT THE RESPONDENT BE ORDERED TO GIVE UP ALL GUNS IN HIS POSSESSION. I AM UNSURE OF HOW MANY FIREARMS HE HAS, BUT KNOW THAT HE HAS A .22 CALIBER PISTOL AND RIFLE.

16. I request that copies of orders be given to the following law enforcement agencies:

Law Enforcement Agency	Address
SANTA BARBARA POLICE DEPARTMENT	303 CABRILLO STREET SANTA BARBARA, CA 93101
SANTA BARBARA SHERIFF'S DEPT.	203 CAMINO PESCADERO ISLA VISTA, CA 93101

17. ☒ I request that time for service of the Order to Show Cause and accompanying papers be shortened so that they may be served no less than *(specify number)*: 2   days before the date set for the hearing. I need to have the order shortening time because of the facts contained in this application. *(Add additional facts if necessary)*:
THE RESPONDENT WILL AVOID BEING SERVED AND I AM AFRAID FOR MY LIFE.

18. ☐ I have been involved in other actions with the restrained person in which restraining orders were issued. *(If known, please specify case numbers or, if available, attach copies of orders)*: _____

19. ☐ I request a court order waiving the fees payable to a law enforcement agency for serving protective orders on the restrained person. A completed Application for Waiver of Court Fees and Costs is filed with this application.

I declare under penalty of perjury under the laws of the State of California that the foregoing is true and correct.

Date: 08-03-95

CATHERINE J. LYNCH ....   ▶ _____
(TYPE OR PRINT NAME)   (SIGNATURE OF PERSON TO BE PROTECTED)

Page four of four

1296 (Rev. January 1, 1994)   **APPLICATION AND DECLARATION**
                                     (Domestic Violence Prevention)

(15) Other orders. Here you can ask for any orders that have not been covered on the printed form. They must be related to protecting you from further abuse. For example:

> That Respondent be ordered to maintain any health care insurance he has for the children and myself.

> That Respondent be ordered to return my engagement ring in good condition.

> That Respondent be ordered to give up all guns in his possession. I am unsure of how many he has, but know that he has a .22-caliber pistol and rifle.

You can also use this space to write down a specific visitation schedule if you didn't have enough room in (9)(b)(3) above.

(16) Delivery to police. List the name and address of any law enforcement agency you want to receive a copy of your orders and the clerk will mail them. List all police agencies that cover areas you visit: your residence or shelter, workplace, family, friends, church, meeting places, and so on. Look in the phone book to get any addresses you need.

We strongly recommend that you also hand-carry a copy of your orders to the law enforcement agencies. This way you will know for sure that they have a copy immediately. This is worth doing.

(17) Short notice to Respondent. The law requires Respondent be notified at least 15 days before the date of the hearing. Check this box and insert "2" if you have a good reason for shortening the time for notice. There are two common reasons: Respondent is avoiding you and is therefore difficult to serve, or you are afraid of what he will do when he finds out you are going to court. Shortening time gives him less time to do something to you.

Some judges automatically grant the order, others need a very good reason. Try for 2 days, but don't be surprised if the judge changes it. In Los Angeles, they are likely to change it to 5 days.

In the tiny space at the end of item (17) or on an additional page, explain why you want the judge to shorten the time for notice. For example, "Respondent has gone into hiding and will be difficult to serve;" or, "I am afraid Respondent will attack me when he hears of my action."

(18) Other restraining orders. Check this box if restraining orders have ever been issued between you and Respondent before, even if it was long ago and they have expired. Give the case number if you have it.

(19) Waiver of fees for service by peace officer. If you are broke and you use a sheriff or marshall to serve Respondent, you may be able to save $20 or $30 if you file a set of Fee Waiver forms and if you qualify (*very* broke).

We recommend that you do not use the sheriff or marshall to serve papers (see Chapter 18) because they often take too long.

Get a friend or relative to do it, or hire a professional server. Anyone over 18, and not a party to the action (not listed anywhere on your court forms), can legally serve papers on Respondent.

Date. Fill in the date you sign the form.

Your name. Type or print your name here, exactly as it appears on these forms.

Your signature. Sign where indicated.

This was the hardest form; the rest is downhill.

B. Order to Show Cause and Temporary Restraining Order

Complete this form in every case. It does two essential things:

✦   it tells Respondent the date and time of the hearing and

✦   it contains your temporary orders restraining Respondent until the date of the hearing.

In the Application, you requested certain orders; now you are completing the form which states the actual order to Respondent. The judge might deny or change some of your requested orders—most likely by simply crossing them out and writing in any changes.

After you examine this form, also look at the Order Attachment forms (Chapter 16G). You can borrow language from them for your own orders, or simply fill out any Attachment form you want to use and attach it to this form.

Figure 15B-1: Order to Show Cause and Temporary Order (front)

Caption. Complete items A–H and items 1 and 2 just as you did on the Application.

(I) Hearing date. Leave this blank. The clerk will fill it in with the date, time and department (the courtroom) for your hearing. Ask the clerk how to find where the hearing will be held. Go there and take a look around to get your bearings.

(J) Temporary orders to issue. Check this box *only* if you requested temporary orders on your Application form. The orders that follow will be effective until the date of your hearing.

(3) Basic restraining order. Check this box if you checked (6)(c) on your Application. Copy the information exactly as you have it on the Application.

(4) Kick-out order. Check this box if you requested immediate orders at item (7) on your Application. Make sure you include the address of your residence.

(5) Stay away order. Check this box if you requested immediate orders at item (8) on your Application and copy the information from (8)(a–e) to (5)(a–e) on this form.

Figure 15B-1: Order to Show Cause and Temporary Order (front)

(A)   (B)   (C)   (H)

ATTORNEY OR PARTY WITHOUT ATTORNEY *(Name and Address):*   **TELEPHONE NO.:**   **FOR COURT USE ONLY**
(805) 427-9326

(D)
CATHERINE J. LYNCH,
AKA KATE LYNCH
6625 SUENO APT. B
SANTA BARBARA, CALIFORNIA 93103
ATTORNEY FOR *(Name):* IN PRO PER

(E)
SUPERIOR COURT OF CALIFORNIA, COUNTY OF SANTA BARBARA
STREET ADDRESS: 1100 ANACAPA STREET
MAILING ADDRESS: SANTA BARBARA, CALIFORNIA 93103
CITY AND ZIP CODE:
BRANCH NAME:

(F)
PERSON TO BE PROTECTED: CATHERINE J. LYNCH

PERSON TO BE RESTRAINED: SHAWN F. GALLAGHER

[X] PETITIONER/PLAINTIFF
[ ] RESPONDENT/DEFENDANT
[ ] PETITIONER/PLAINTIFF
[X] RESPONDENT/DEFENDANT

(G)
ORDER TO SHOW CAUSE AND TEMPORARY RESTRAINING ORDER (CLETS)
(Domestic Violence Prevention Act)

CASE NUMBER:
323404

1. PERSON TO BE PROTECTED *(name):* CATHERINE J. LYNCH
   (Insert in item 1 names of all persons to be protected by this order.)

2. PERSON TO BE RESTRAINED *(name):* SHAWN F. GALLAGHER

Sex: [X] M [ ] F Ht.: 6-4 Wt.: 200 Hair Color: BRN Eye Color: BRN Race: WHITE Age: 32 Date of birth: 11-07-62

(I)
To Person to be Restrained:
You have the right to attend the court hearing and oppose the application, with or without an attorney at the date, time, and place shown in the box below to give any legal reason why the orders sought in the attached application should not be granted. If you do not attend the court hearing, the court may grant the requested orders, which may last up to 3 years without further notice to you.

Date: Time: Dept.:   Room:

TEMPORARY RESTRAINING ORDER

(J)
This order shall expire at the date and the time of the hearing shown in the box above unless extended by the court.

[X] UNTIL THE TIME OF HEARING, IT IS ORDERED
3. [X] Person to be restrained shall not contact, molest, attack, strike, threaten, sexually assault, batter, telephone, or disturb the peace of the person to be protected [ ] and the following family and household members *(names):*

4. [X] Person to be restrained must immediately move from *(address):*
   and take only personal clothing and effects needed until the hearing.

5. [X] Person to be restrained is ordered to stay at least *(specify):*   yards away from the person to be protected and the following persons and places *(the addresses of these places are optional and you do not have to reveal them):*
   a. [ ] Protected person's family and household members *(name):*
   b. [X] Protected person's residence *(address optional):* 6625 SUENO APT. B S.B., CA
   c. [X] Protected person's place of work *(address optional):*
   d. [X] The children's school or place of child care *(address optional):*
   e. [X] Other *(specify):* PETITIONER'S SISTER, ANN LYNCH'S HOUSE
      (address optional): 6592 SABADO TARDE, SANTA BARBARA, CA

Violation of this temporary restraining order is a misdemeanor, punishable by a $1,000 fine, one year in jail, or both or may be punishable as a felony. This order shall be enforced by all law enforcement officers in the State of California. Penal Code section 12021g prohibits any person subject to a restraining order from purchasing or attempting to purchase or otherwise obtain a firearm. Such conduct is subject to a $1,000 fine and imprisonment.

(Temporary Restraining Order continued on reverse)

Form Adopted by Rule 1296.10
Judicial Council of California
1296.10 (Rev. January 1, 1994)

ORDER TO SHOW CAUSE AND
TEMPORARY RESTRAINING ORDER (CLETS)
(Domestic Violence Prevention)

Family Code § 6200 et seq.

Figure 15B-2: Order to Show Cause and Temporary Order (back)

(A) Short caption. Type in the names of the parties, exactly as entered in the caption on page 1, but omit aliases (AKA), if any.

(B) Case number. Leave it blank; the clerk will stamp your case number when you file your forms.

(6) Custody. Check this box if you requested immediate orders at item (9) on your Application. List the names of your children (remember, we are only talking about children who are the biological or legal children of Respondent) for whom you requested sole custody.

(7) Property control. Check this box if you requested immediate orders at item (11) on your Application. List the property you for which you requested exclusive use.

(8) Other orders. Check this box if you checked box (15) on your Application. This time, instead of writing a request, you are writing an order. For example, if you requested that "Respondent return my engagement ring undamaged," you would now write, "Respondent is ordered to return Petitioner's engagement ring undamaged."

(9) Delivery to police. Check this box and (9)(a) and (9)(c). List all the police agencies you listed in (16) of your Application.

(10) Waiver of fees. Check this box only if you checked (19) on your Application and filed completed Fee Waiver forms.

(11) Short notice to Respondent. Check this box if you checked box (17) on the Application and enter the number of days you entered there for the shortened time for service.

(11)(a–f) Documents to be served on Respondent. You must serve Respondent with a copy of every form indicated here. (11)(c) is a blank form, that Respondent can use to enter the case and tell his side.

> **(a–c) To be served in every case.** These are the forms you are required to serve on Respondent in every case.

> **(d–f) Optional documents.** Check boxes to indicate which of the listed forms you will be filing with your Application. Copies of these must also be served on Respondent.

> **(f) Other documents.** Check this box and type in the names of any forms you will be filing with your Application that were not mentioned above. For example: Wage Assignment Order, Ex Parte Declaration re: Notice, Certificate of Assignment.

Leave the rest of this form blank.

Figure 15B-2: Order to Show Cause and Temporary Order (back)

Ⓐ   Ⓑ

| PERSON TO BE PROTECTED (Name): CATHERINE J. LYNCH
PERSON TO BE RESTRAINED (Name): SHAWN F. GALLAGHER | CASE NUMBER: 323404 |

6. [X] Care, custody, and control of the following minor children are temporarily awarded to protected person:

         Child's name
         RALPH L. GALLAGHER

7. [X] Exclusive temporary use, possession, and control of the following property are given to protected person:
     1976 RED VOLKSWAGON CONVERTIBLE, LIC #1EU2U021

8. [X] OTHER ORDERS (specify): 1. RESPONDENT IS ORDERED TO MAINTAIN ANY AND ALL HEALTH INSURANCE COVERAGE ON BOTH THE PETITIONER AND RALPH L. GALLAGHER.
     2. THE RESPONDENT IS ORDERED TO TURN OVER ALL FIREAMRS IN POSSESSION TO THE SANTA BARBARA POLICE DEPTARTMENT.

9. [X] By the close of business on the date of this order a copy of this order and any proof of service shall be given to the law enforcement agencies listed below as follows:
     a. [X] Protected person shall deliver.
     b. [ ] Protected person's attorney shall deliver.
     c. [X] The clerk of the court shall mail.

Law enforcement agency	Address
SANTA BARBARA POLICE DEPARTMENT	303 CABRILLO ST. S.B. CA.
SANTA BARBARA SHERIFF'S DEPT.	203 CAMINO PESCADERO ISLA VISTA, CA

10. [ ] Fees for service of this order by law enforcement agencies are waived.

11. [X] Application for an order shortening time is granted and the following documents shall be personally served on the defendant no less than (specify number): 2   days before the time set for hearing:
     a. Order to Show Cause and Temporary Restraining Order (Domestic Violence Prevention)
     b. Application and Declaration (Domestic Violence Prevention)
     c. Blank Responsive Declaration (Domestic Violence Prevention)
     d. [ ] Income and Expense Declaration
     e. [ ] Declaration Under Uniform Custody of Minors Act
     f. [ ] Other (specify):

Date: ▶ _____
                                     JUOGE OF THE SUPERIOR COURT

This order is effective when made. It is enforceable anywhere in California by any law enforcement agency that has received the order, is shown a copy of it, or has verified its existence on the California Law Enforcement Telecommunications System (CLETS).
If proof of service on the restrained person has not been received, and the restrained person was not present at the court hearing, the law enforcement agency shall advise the restrained person of the terms of the order and then shall enforce it.

(SEAL)	**CLERK'S CERTIFICATE**
	I certify that the foregoing Order to Show Cause and Temporary Restraining Order (CLETS) is a true and correct copy of the original on file in the court.
	Date: Clerk, by _____ , Deputy

1296.10 (Rev. January 1, 1994)
                 ORDER TO SHOW CAUSE AND
             TEMPORARY RESTRAINING ORDER (CLETS)   Page two
                   (Domestic Violence Prevention)

C. Restraining Order After Hearing

Complete this form in every case. This is the form the judge will use when she decides to issue restraining orders after hearing both sides at the hearing. These restraining orders will then be in effect for up to three years from the date of the hearing.

After you examine this form, also look at the Order Attachment forms (Chapter 16G). You can borrow language from them for your own orders, or simply fill out any Attachment form you want to use and attach it to this form.

Figure 15C-1: Restraining Order After Hearing (front)

Caption. Complete items A–H exactly as you did on the Application.

(1) Hearing details. Unless the clerk fills this in for you, leave it blank until the date of the hearing.

(2)(a-b) Who's there. Leave this blank until after you have been to the court hearing.

(3) Who's who.

(a) **Respondent.** Fill this out exactly as you did in item (2) of your Application.

(b) **Protected person.** Enter your name exactly it appears in item (1) of your Application.

(c) **Others protected.** Enter the names of any other protected persons exactly they appear in item (1) of your Application.

Date order expires. Leave this blank. The clerk will fill it in after the hearing.

(4) Restraining orders

(a) **Basic order.** Check this box if you checked item (6) on your Application. Copy the information exactly as you have it on the Application.

(b) **Stay-away order.** Check this box if you checked item (8) on your Application and copy the information from (8)(b–e) to (4)(b)(1–4) on this form.

(c) **Kick-out order.** Check this box if you checked item (7) on your Application. Make sure you include the address of your residence.

Figure 15C-2: Restraining Order After Hearing (back)

(A) Short caption. Type in the names of the parties, exactly as entered in the caption on page 1, but omit aliases (AKA), if any.

(B) Case number. Leave it blank; the clerk will stamp your case number when you file your forms.

(5) Custody and visitation. Fill out this section exactly as you did in item (9) of your Application. If you chose "supervised visitation," state exactly how that supervision is to be arranged. You can borrow language from special orders the section below.

Figure 15C-1: Restraining Order After Hearing (front)

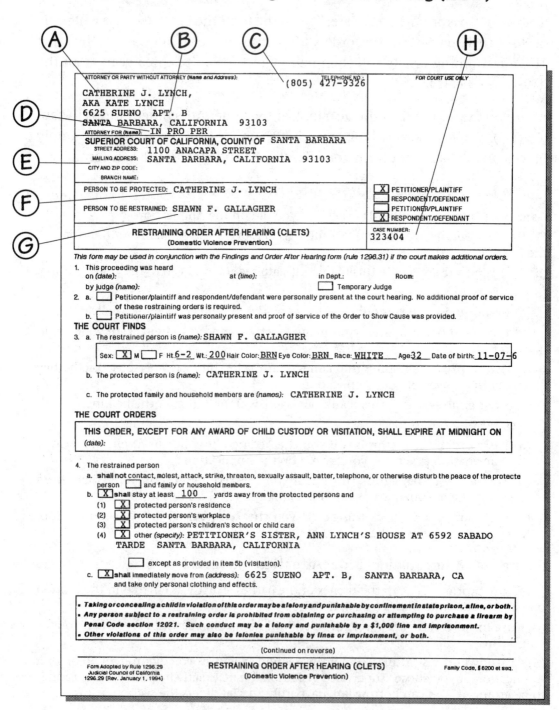

Special orders. In section D, below, you will find orders for four different custody and visitation situations. These examples may help you find language for your own orders.

Additional page: If you can't fit your custody and visitation order in the space provided, attach one or more additional pages as described in Chapter 16A.

(6) Fee for service waived. Check this box if you checked box (19) on the Application.

(7) Service on police near your residence. Fill in the name of the police station of sheriff's office nearest to where you live. You have to deliver to them a copy of this order before the end of the day the orders were issued. If Respondent was not at the hearing, you must return later to give them a copy of the Proof of Service form to let them know that he has been served.

(8) Additional police agencies. Check this box, and check box (8)(1) and (8)(3). Then copy the information you listed in item (16) of your Application. It is important to hand deliver copies of this Order and Proof of Service to these police agencies even though the clerk will also mail them a copy. It makes the agencies immediately aware of your protective order.

(9) Other orders. Copy item (8) from your Order To Show Cause and Temporary Restraining Order form. If you requested child support, type in the order but leave the amount blank so the clerk can fill it in at the hearing.

Leave the rest of the form blank.

If you don't have children and are not asking the court to reimburse you for any out-of-pocket expenses associated with obtaining the restraining order, you can skip to Chapter 17.

Special custody and visitation orders

Below are examples of orders to fit four special custody and visitation situations that were discussed in Chapter 11 (sections 1-3). Use them for ideas for language that will suit your own situation.

Order 1. Children left behind

Petitioner and Respondent shall have joint legal custody of the minor children, Louis, born _____, age 7, and Ivan, born _____, age 10, and Respondent shall have primary physical custody. Petitioner shall have the physical care and custody of the minor children commencing Friday, July 28, 1995, at 3:30 pm until Monday, July 31, 1995, until 9:00 am and every alternate weekend thereafter. Petitioner shall also have the children for the first ten weeks each of summer school vacation each year, all of the school spring break at Easter, and the first part of the children's Christmas holiday beginning at the end of the last day of school and ending noon Christmas Day in even years and the second part of the children's Christmas holiday starting noon Christmas Day and ending the first day of school in odd years. The children shall be picked up from school and returned to school by Petitioner, and on Christmas Day the children shall be picked up from or delivered to the home of Respondent. The parties shall have no contact other than to confirm or cancel visitation plans. Both parties shall be entitled

Figure 15C-2: Restraining Order After Hearing (back)

Ⓐ   Ⓑ

PERSON TO BE PROTECTED *(Name):* CATHERINE J. LYNCH	CASE NUMBER: 323404
PERSON TO BE RESTRAINED *(Name):* SHAWN F. GALLAGHER	

5. a. [X] Custody of the minor children

Child's name	Physical custody is awarded to *(specify name of parent or "joint")*	Legal custody is awarded to *(specify name of parent or "joint")*
(1) RALPH L GALLAGHER	CATHERINE J. LYNCH	CATHERINE J. LYNCH
(2)		
(3)		
(4)		
(5)		
(6)		

b. Parent without physical custody *(name):* SHAWN F. GALLAGHER

   (1) [ ] shall not have visitation

   (2) [X] shall have visitation as follows *(specify times and conditions, if any):*
VISITATION SHALL BE EVERY SUNDAY AT 1:00 P.M. TO MONDAY AT 5:00 P.M. THE CHILD SHALL BE PICKED-UP AND DROPPED-OFF AT THE SANTA BARBARA POLICE DEPARTMENT LOCATED AT 303 CABRILLO STREET SANTA BARBARA, CA

6. [ ] Fees for service of this order by law enforcement agencies are waived.

7. By the close of judicial business on the date of this order, a copy of this order shall be delivered by the protected person to th law enforcement agency having jurisdiction over the residence of the protected person, who shall provide information to assist i identifying the restrained person. Proof of service of this order on the restrained person shall also be provided to the law enforcemen agency unless the order shows the restrained person was present in court. The law enforcement agency having jurisdiction ove the plaintiff's residence is *(name and address of agency):*
SANTA BARBARA POLICE DEPARTMENT 303 CABRILLO STREET SANTA BARBARA, CA

8. [ ] A copy of this order shall be given to the additional law enforcement agencies listed below as follows:

   (1) [X] Person to be protected shall delivery.   (2) [ ] Person to be protected's attorney shall deliver.

   (3) [X] The clerk of the court shall mail.

Law enforcement agency	Address
SANTA BARBARA POLICE DEPARTMENT	303 CABRILLO STREET S.B., CA
SANTA BARBARA SHERIFF'S DEPT.	203 CAMINO PESCADERO S.B., CA

9. Other orders *(specify):* 1. THE RESPONDENT IS ORDERED TO MAINTAIN ANY AND ALL HEALTH INS. COVERAGE ON BOTH PETITIONER AND RALPH L GALLAGHER; 2. RESPONDENT TO TURN OVER ALL FIREARMS TO S.B.P.D.; 3. CHILD SUPPORT IN AMOUNT OF $____ MO.

Date: _____ ▶ _____

                                                     JUDGE OF THE SUPERIOR COURT

This order is effective when made. It is enforceable anywhere in California by any law enforcement agency that has received the order, is shown a copy of it, or has verified its existence on the California Law Enforcement Telecommunications System (CLETS).
If proof of service on the restrained person has not been received, and the restrained person was not present at the court hearing, the law enforcement agency shall advise the restrained person of the terms of the order and then shall enforce it.

(SEAL)

CLERK'S CERTIFICATE

I certify that the foregoing Restraining Order After Hearing (CLETS) is a true and correct copy of the original on file in the court.

Date: _____   Clerk, by _____ , Deputy

1296.29 (Rev. January 1, 1994)   **RESTRAINING ORDER AFTER HEARING (CLETS)**   Page two
                                           (Domestic Violence Prevention)

to all school records and shall be permitted to attend all school conferences, performances and other school activities. Other than for emergency medical treatment, both parties shall consent to extraordinary medical treatment. Respondent shall schedule and take the children to routine medical checkups.

Order 2. Monitored visitation, no contact, infant

Commencing July 1, 1995, Petitioner shall have primary legal and physical custody of the minor child, Patricia Smith, born 1/1/95, and Respondent may have monitored visits with the minor child in the home of Petitioner's mother from 10 am to 12 noon on Wednesday, Saturday and Sunday each week. When the minor child attains the age of 24 months the Saturday and Sunday visits may be extended to three hours from 10 am to 1:00 pm. All visits shall be monitored by Petitioner's mother, or any other responsible adult selected by Petitioner in her sole discretion. If Petitioner selects a professional monitor, Respondent shall pay the cost of same in advance of each visit. If the monitor is not paid in advance, the visit shall not take place. Respondent shall not remove the minor child from the home of Petitioner's mother during these visits, or attempt to contact the minor child at any times other than these designated visits for a period of three years. When the minor child attains the age of three years the visitation schedule shall be reviewed by the parties and/or the court if the parties cannot mutually agree on a modified visitation schedule to accommodate the age of the child and the status of the parties at that time. Respondent shall not contact Petitioner for any purpose other than to leave a telephone message on her answering machine to confirm or cancel the visitation.

Note that this order is for a six-month-old infant. Courts are inclined to order frequent, short visits for an infant. An older child can tolerate longer spaces between visits, and longer visits.

Order 3. Neutral pick-up and drop-off

Commencing January 1, 1998, Petitioner shall have sole legal and physical custody of the minor child, Harriet Smith, born 1/1/95, and Respondent shall have visitation with the minor child commencing Friday January 3, 1998, from 3:30 pm on Friday until 9:00 am on Monday, and in alternate weeks thereafter. Respondent shall pick up the minor child from preschool on Friday, and shall deliver her to preschool on Monday. Respondent shall have no contact with the Petitioner except to confirm or cancel the visitation. Respondent shall have no contact with the minor child except on his days of visitation; provided, however, Respondent may attend school functions for all parents, and telephone the minor child between the hours of 6:00 pm and 8:00 pm each evening. Respondent may have installed a telephone in the child's room for purposes of these phone calls and pay the telephone bill for same. Said telephone is to be used for no purpose other than to facilitate Respondent's communication with the minor child. Each party shall maintain clothes and toys for the minor child so that neither party is obligated to transfer clothes or toys to the other parent. The child shall have two transfer outfits which shall be used for pick-up and drop-off days, and the parties shall share the cost of same equally. Petitioner's home and work telephone numbers and addresses shall remain confidential, and Respondent shall call Petitioner at the following phone number to confirm or cancel each visit at least 24 hours in advance of same by recorded message.

Order 4. Special needs

The court finds that the minor child has been diagnosed as autistic and is enrolled in a special day program for autistic children. She also requires special care at home. The court finds that these extra expenses are $900 a month, and commencing January 1, 1995, and on the first day of each month thereafter, Respondent shall pay to Petitioner the amount of $450 per month in addition to the child support ordered herein to assist with these expenses. These payments shall continue until child support terminates.

D. Declaration Re Ex Parte Notice

Complete this form in every case, whether or not you are requesting temporary orders. This declaration tells the judge one of four things:

(1) when and how you gave Respondent notice of your request for ex parte temporary orders; or

(2) what you did to try to reach Respondent and why you couldn't; or

(3) why it is necessary to get temporary orders without telling Respondent about it first; or

(4) that you are not requesting temporary orders, so it is therefore not necessary to give Respondent notice at this time.

There is no statewide form for this declaration, so we use a copy of the blank Declaration form (Chapter 16E) for this job. However, if your county has their own local form for this purpose, that's the one you should use. Ask the clerk. Any local form is sure to use the same information we provide here.

Figure 15D: Declaration Re Ex Parte Notice

Caption. Complete items A–H exactly as you did on the Application.

Heading. Just under the caption, type:

"DECLARATION RE EX PARTE NOTICE"

Statement. Type in a statement similar to one of the following four examples:

(1) Respondent notified

On 8/3/99, at 8 am, I contacted Respondent (personally/by telephone) and advised him that on 8/4/99, I would be appearing before the court to request temporary restraining orders against him, and I gave him the address of the court.

(2) Unable to contact Respondent

I attempted to contact the Respondent by telephone at his home and at his workplace on 8/2/99 and 8/3/99. I made five attempts each day. I do not know how else to reach him.

(3) Respondent not notified for a good reason

Respondent has threatened to beat me and take the children if I do anything against him. I am afraid that he will hurt me and take the children if he hears about this action before temporary orders are granted.

(4) Temporary orders not requested

I am not requesting temporary orders at this time.

Date and sign. At the bottom of the form, type in the date, type in your full name, sign on the signature line, and check the box "Petitioner/Plaintiff" below the line.

Figure 15D: Declaration Re Ex Parte Notice

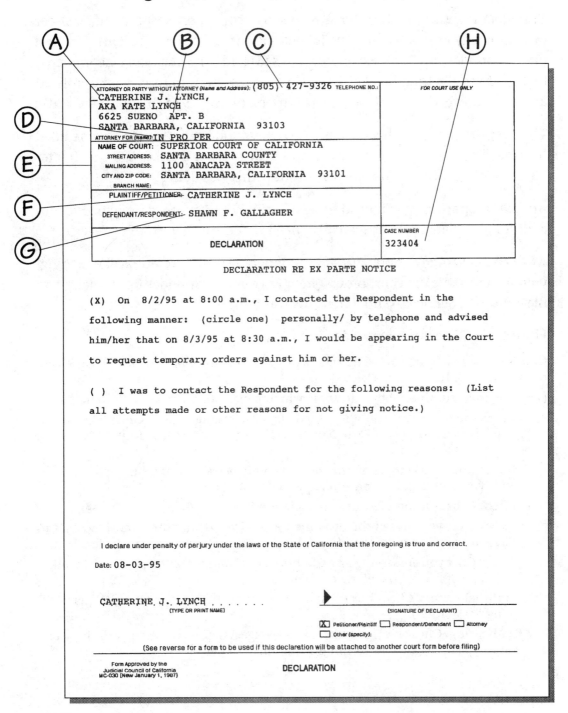

(A) (B) (C) (H)

ATTORNEY OR PARTY WITHOUT ATTORNEY *(Name and Address):* (805) 427-9326 TELEPHONE NO.:
CATHERINE J. LYNCH,
AKA KATE LYNCH
6625 SUENO   APT. B
SANTA BARBARA, CALIFORNIA 93103

FOR COURT USE ONLY

(D) ATTORNEY FOR *(Name):* IN PRO PER
NAME OF COURT: SUPERIOR COURT OF CALIFORNIA
STREET ADDRESS: SANTA BARBARA COUNTY
(E) MAILING ADDRESS: 1100 ANACAPA STREET
CITY AND ZIP CODE: SANTA BARBARA, CALIFORNIA   93101
BRANCH NAME:

(F) PLAINTIFF/PETITIONER: CATHERINE J. LYNCH

DEFENDANT/RESPONDENT: SHAWN F. GALLAGHER

(G)

DECLARATION

CASE NUMBER
323404

DECLARATION RE EX PARTE NOTICE

(X) On 8/2/95 at 8:00 a.m., I contacted the Respondent in the following manner: (circle one) personally/ by telephone and advised him/her that on 8/3/95 at 8:30 a.m., I would be appearing in the Court to request temporary orders against him or her.

( ) I was to contact the Respondent for the following reasons: (List all attempts made or other reasons for not giving notice.)

I declare under penalty of perjury under the laws of the State of California that the foregoing is true and correct.

Date: 08-03-95

CATHERINE J. LYNCH
(TYPE OR PRINT NAME)

▶

(SIGNATURE OF DECLARANT)

[X] Petitioner/Plaintiff [ ] Respondent/Defendant [ ] Attorney
[ ] Other (specify):

(See reverse for a form to be used if this declaration will be attached to another court form before filing)

Form Approved by the
Judicial Council of California
MC-030 [New January 1, 1987]

DECLARATION

E. Proof of Service

This form is signed by the person who serves papers on Respondent to swear under penalty of perjury that the job was done correctly at a certain time and place. Complete the form except for items (3) and (5) which will be completed by the server. If a friend makes service, you can wait until service is completed and type in everything. Always keep extra blank copies of this form around.

The first time you use this form is to give Respondent notice of the scheduled hearing. The papers that get served and how to do it is described in Chapter 18. A Proof of Service must be filed to show this was done.

Additional papers. If you need to serve Respondent another time to give him additional declarations, you will also need to file another Proof of Service.

After the hearing (Chapter 20). If Respondent was not present at the hearing, you need to serve the court orders (item (1)(g)) on Respondent personally and file a Proof of Service to show that this was done.

Figure 15E-1: Proof of Service

Caption. Complete items A–G exactly as you did on the Application. Add the case number at item H.

(1) Papers served. Check boxes to show which papers were served on Respondent.

The first time. In every case, check boxes (a), (b), (c) and (g). Also check box (h) and type in: Declaration re Ex Parte Notice. Only if you used those forms, also check boxes (d), (e) and (f).

Check (d) if you completed the Income and Expense Declaration. Also check (h) and type in "blank Income and Expense Declaration."

Check (e) if you completed the Declaration Under UCCJA.

Check (f) if you missed the deadline for service the first time and have had to have the court set a new hearing date and extend your temporary orders.

Check (h) if you are serving any additional Declarations and type in "Declaration of (name of person(s) making declaration)."

Additional papers. Check box (h) and type in "Declaration of (name(s) of person(s) making declaration)."

After hearing. Check box (g). If there was a Wage Assignment Order, also check box (h) and type in "Wage and Earnings Assignment Order."

Figure 15E: Proof of Service

ATTORNEY OR PARTY WITHOUT ATTORNEY *(Name and Address)*: (805) 427-9326 TELEPHONE NO.:

CATHERINE J. LYNCH,
AKA KATE LYNCH
6625 SUENO APT. B
SANTA BARBARA, CALIFORNIA 93103

ATTORNEY FOR *(Name)*: IN PRO PER

SUPERIOR COURT OF CALIFORNIA, COUNTY OF SANTA BARBARA

STREET ADDRESS: 1100 ANACAPA STREET

MAILING ADDRESS: SANTA BARBARA, CALIFORNIA 93103

CITY AND ZIP CODE:

BRANCH NAME:

PLAINTIFF: CATHERINE J. LYNCH

DEFENDANT: SHAWN F. GALLAGHER

FOR COURT USE ONLY

CASE NUMBER: 323404

PROOF OF SERVICE

PERSONAL SERVICE

Instruction: *After having the other party served with a copy of the document identified in item 1, attach a completed Proof of Service to the original or to a true copy of the original and give it to the clerk for filing. Neither the plaintiff nor the defendant can serve these papers.*

1. I served a copy of the following documents *(check the box before the title of each document you served)*:

DOMESTIC VIOLENCE

a. [X] Order to Show Cause and Temporary Restraining Order (Domestic Violence Prevention - Uniform Parentage)

b. [X] Application and Declaration (Domestic Violence Prevention - Uniform Parentage)

c. [X] Blank Responsive Declaration (Domestic Violence Prevention - Uniform Parentage)

d. [ ] Income and Expense Declaration

e. [ ] Declaration Under Uniform Custody of Minors Act

f. [ ] Application and Order for Re-issuance of Order to Show Cause (Domestic Violence Prevention - Uniform Parentage - Family Law)

g. [ ] Order After Hearing (Family Law - Domestic Violence Prevention - Uniform Parentage)

h. [ ] Other *(specify)*:

HARASSMENT

i. [ ] Order to Show Cause and Temporary Restraining Order

j. [ ] Petition for Injunction Prohibiting Harassment

k. [ ] Blank Response to Petition for Injunction Prohibiting Harassment

l. [ ] Other *(specify)*:

EMANCIPATION

m. [ ] Petition for Declaration of Emancipation

n. [ ] Petition for Recission of Declaration of Emancipation

PARENTAGE

o. [ ] Complaint to Establish Parental Relationship (Uniform Parentage Act)

OTHER

p. [ ] *(Specify)*:

2. Person served *(name)*: SHAWN F. GALLAGHER AKA P.P. GALLAGHER

3. By personally delivering copies to the person served, as follows:
   (1) Date: 08-03-95   (2) Time: 11:30 AM
   (3) Address: 6435 GOLDEN GATE AVENUE
   SANTA BARBARA, CALIFORNIA 93103

4. At the time of service I was at least 18 years of age and **not a party to this cause.**

5. I declare under penalty of perjury under the laws of the State of California that the foregoing is true and correct.
   Date: AUGUST 3, 1995

   ANNE ACKERMAN
   · · · · · · · · · · · · · · ·
   (TYPE OR PRINT NAME)   (SIGNATURE)

(See reverse for proof of service by mail)

Form Approved by Rule 1296.40
Judicial Council of California
1296.40 (Rev. January 1, 1985)

PROOF OF SERVICE

(2) Person served. Type in Respondent's name as entered in the caption.

(3) Details of service. Enter the date, the time, and the address where service was accomplished. This information can be entered by hand (printed clearly with a black ballpoint pen) after service is actually accomplished, or you can type it in before it gets signed.

(5) Oath and signature. You can type in the date and name of the person signing, or it can be filled in by hand at the time of signing (in very neat printing with a black ballpoint pen).

Chapter 16

Other forms you may need

A. Additional Page

Whenever you need more room to complete an item on any form, type "See Attachment A (or B or C, etc.)" at the item, then put your information on the Additional Page form as described below. Make extra copies of the form in the book so you will always have a blank one available.

To use the form, type in the caption and add the case number, if you have it. On the first line, centered and in capital letters, type the name of the form and the identity of the item you are completing, like this: "APPLICATION AND DECLARATION, ATTACHMENT A." Then complete your information. If you need more than one page, use a blank sheet or another Additional Page with the heading "APPLICATION AND DECLARATION, ATTACHMENT A (continued)."

Figure 16A: Additional Page

(A) **Short caption.** Type in the names of the parties, exactly as entered in the other captions, but omit any aliases.

(B) **Case number.** Type in the case number if one has already been issued, otherwise leave it blank and the clerk will add it when you file your documents.

(C) **Heading.** Type in the name of the form and the identity of the item you are completing, for example: RESTRAINING ORDER AFTER HEARING, ATTACHMENT B.

(D) **Page number.** Indicate which page in order this is and the total number of pages added, for example: "Page 1 of 1," or "Page 2 of 4."

Fig. 16A: Additional Page

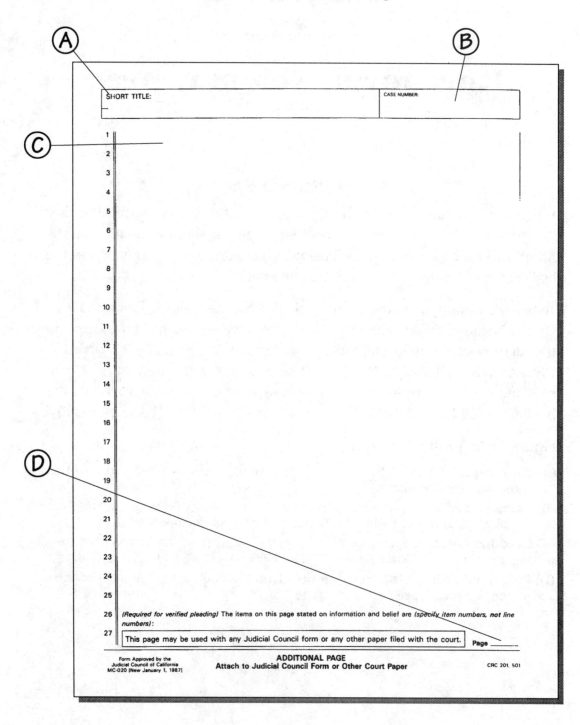

B. Declaration Under Uniform Child Custody Jurisdiction Act (UCCJA)

This form must be filed only if you checked box (5)(c)(5) on the Application and Declaration (Chapter 15A).

Figure 16B-1: Declaration Under UCCJA (front)

Caption. Complete items A–H exactly as you did on the Application. Add the word "and" before Respondent's name.

(2) Confidential addresses. Check this box if your address and the address of the children is confidential and not used on any of your other forms. Do not enter any addresses.

(3) Number of children subject to the proceeding. Type in the number of minor children listed on the Application at item (5)(b).

    (3a) Information for first child. Complete the requested information for the oldest child on your list. Notice that the residence information covers the past five years.

    (3b) Information for second child. If there's a second child, complete the requested information for the next oldest child on your list. Notice that there's a box you can check if the residence information is the same as for the first child.

    (3c) Information for additional children. If there are more children, check this box and give the same information for each additional child on an Additional Page form with the heading: DECLARATION UNDER UCCJA: ATTACHMENT 3C. Add as

Figure 16B-1: Declaration Under UCCJA (front)

Ⓐ   Ⓑ   Ⓒ   Ⓗ

Ⓓ Ⓔ Ⓕ Ⓖ

ATTORNEY OR PARTY WITHOUT ATTORNEY (Name and Address):   TELEPHONE NO.: (805) 427-9326   FOR COURT USE ONLY

CATHERINE J. LYNCH,
AKA KATE LYNCH
6625 SUENO APT. B
SANTA BARBARA, CALIFORNIA 93103
ATTORNEY FOR (Name): IN PRO PER

SUPERIOR COURT OF CALIFORNIA, COUNTY OF SANTA BARBARA
STREET ADDRESS: 1100 ANACAPA STREET
MAILING ADDRESS: SANTA BARBARA, CALIFORNIA 93103
CITY AND ZIP CODE:
BRANCH NAME:
CASE NAME: In Re LYNCH AND GALLAGHER

DECLARATION UNDER
UNIFORM CHILD CUSTODY JURISDICTION ACT (UCCJA)

CASE NUMBER: 323404

1. **I am a party** to this proceeding to determine custody of a child.
2. ☐ Declarant's present address is not disclosed. It is confidential under Civil Code section 5158. The address of children presently residing with declarant is identified on this declaration as confidential.
3. (Number): ONE minor children are subject to this proceeding as follows:
   (Insert the information requested below. The residence information must be given for the last FIVE years.)

a. Child's name		Place of birth SANTA BARBARA	Date of birth 12-17-90	Sex M
Period of residence	Address 6625 SUENO APT. B SANTA BARBARA, CA ☐ Confidential	Person child lived with (name and present address) CATHERINE J. LYNCH 6625 SUENO APT. B SANTA BARBARA CA		Relationship MOTHER
1993 to present				
1990 to 1993	1400 STEAMBOAT LANE RENO, NEVADA 99876	SUSAN GALLAGHER 1400 STEAMBOAT LANE RENO, NEVADO 99876		G-MOTHER
to				
to				
to				

b. Child's name		Place of birth	Date of birth	Sex
☐ Residence information is the same as given above for child a. (If NOT the same, provide the information below.)				
Period of residence	Address	Person child lived with (name and present address)		Relationship
to present	☐ Confidential			
to				
to				

c. ☐ Additional children are listed on Attachment 3c. (Provide requested information for additional children on an attachment.)
(Continued on reverse)

Form Approved by the
Judicial Council of California
MC-150 (Rev. January 1, 1993)
   DECLARATION UNDER
UNIFORM CHILD CUSTODY JURISDICTION ACT (UCCJA)
   Civil Code, § 5158
Probate Code, §§ 1510(f), 1512

many pages as necessary to cover all children on your list.

Figure 16B-2: Declaration Under UCCJA (back)

(A) Caption. Type in the names of the parties.

(4) Participation in court action regarding custody of a child. Did you take part in any capacity in a court action anywhere, any time, regarding custody of a child listed on this form?

> Check "No" if you did not. Skip to (5).

> Check "Yes" if you did, then complete (4a–d).

(4a) Names. Type the names of each child involved.

(4b) Your role. Check a box to indicate if you were involved in the proceeding as a party, witness or some other capacity. If other, describe.

(4c) Court. Type in the name and address of the court.

(4d) Orders. Give the date of the court order. If no order, type in "none."

(5) Aware of court action regarding custody of a child. Are you aware of any court action anywhere, any time, regarding custody of a child listed on this form?

> Check "No" if you did not. Skip to (6).

> Check "Yes" if you did, then complete (5)(a–d).

(5a) Names. Type the names of each child involved.

(5b) Nature of action. Check to indicate if it was a divorce, guardianship, adoption or other. If other, describe it.

(5c) Court. Type in the name and address of the court.

(5d) Status. Is the action pending or completed? Briefly state results.

(6) Other people claiming custody or visitation rights. Are you aware of anyone not a party to this case who claims any right to custody or visitation with any child listed on this form?

> Check "No" if you do not know of such a person. Skip to the oath.

> Check "Yes" if you do know of such a person, then complete (6a–c) giving the requested information about each person who claims custody or visitation rights with any child listed on this form.

> **Oath.** Type in the date of signing and type in your name (as it appears on all the forms) on the dotted line to the left of the signature line.

(7) Attached pages. If you attach any pages to this form, check this box and indicate how many pages are attached.

Figure 16B-2: Declaration Under UCCJA (back)

Ⓐ

SHORT TITLE: In re LYNCH & GALLAGHER	CASE NUMBER: 323404

4. Have you participated as a party or a witness or in some other capacity in another litigation or custody proceeding, in California or elsewhere, concerning custody of a child subject to this proceeding?

   [X] No ☐ Yes *(If yes, provide the following information:)*

   a. Name of each child:

   b. Capacity of declarant: ☐ party ☐ witness ☐ other *(specify):*
   c. Court *(specify name, state, location):*

   d. Court order or judgment *(date):*

5. Do you have information about a custody proceeding pending in a California court or any other court concerning a child subject to this proceeding, other than that stated in item 4?

   [X] No ☐ Yes *(If yes, provide the following information:)*

   a. Name of each child:

   b. Nature of proceeding: ☐ dissolution or divorce ☐ guardianship ☐ adoption ☐ other *(specify):*

   c. Court *(specify name, state, location):*

   d. Status of proceeding:

6. Do you know of any person who is not a party to this proceeding who has physical custody or claims to have custody of or visitation rights with any child subject to this proceeding?

   [X] No ☐ Yes *(If yes, provide the following information:)*

a. Name and address of person	b. Name and address of person	c. Name and address of person
☐ Has physical custody ☐ Claims custody rights ☐ Claims visitation rights	☐ Has physical custody ☐ Claims custody rights ☐ Claims visitation rights	☐ Has physical custody ☐ Claims custody rights ☐ Claims visitation rights
Name of each child	Name of each child	Name of each child

I declare under penalty of perjury under the laws of the State of California that the foregoing is true and correct.

Date: 08-03-95

CATHERINE J. LYNCH . . . .   ▶
(TYPE OR PRINT NAME)   (SIGNATURE OF DECLARANT)

7. ☐ Number of pages attached after this page:

NOTICE TO DECLARANT:	You have a continuing duty to inform this court if you obtain any information about a custody proceeding in a California court or any other court concerning a child subject to this proceeding.

MC-150 (Rev. January 1, 1993)   **DECLARATION UNDER
UNIFORM CHILD CUSTODY JURISDICTION ACT (UCCJA)**   Page two

C. Income and Expense Declarations

This set of forms is required *only* if you and the abuser have minor children and you are requesting an order for child support. Otherwise, do *not* file the I and E forms, even if you are asking for attorney fees. You don't want the abuser to have your private financial information if you can avoid it.

The Application form says (just above item 10) to file the I and E forms if you are asking for attorney fees. Yes, this is good law for a family action, but *not* in a DVRO case. In a family action, an award for attorney fees depends on need and ability to pay (Family Code §2030) so you do need the I and E forms. But in a DVRO case, attorney fees can be awarded to the prevailing party (Family Code §6344) without consideration of need or ability to pay. The I and E forms are not relevant. If you run into a judge who doesn't get this, read him this information and tell him you don't want the Respondent to have access to your private financial information.

Figure 16C-1: Income and Expense Declaration

This cover sheet includes information drawn from the following three or four forms, so it will be easier if you do this one last.

Caption. Complete items A–H exactly as you did on the Application.

Step 1: Attachments. Just under the caption, check boxes to show which additional pages are attached. Always check the first two boxes (Income and Expense forms) and check the third box if you are asking for child support.

Step 2: Information about you. These items are easy to understand. Give the requested information at items (1–6). Item (6): Note that the total number of minors you are obligated to support includes all of your children, not just the ones you have with the abuser.

Step 3: Monthly income. Enter the requested information. Item (8)—taken from item (16b) of the Income Information form—is your current net monthly income. Item (7), taken from item (16a), is your average over the past 12 months. If the two are different, explain why on this form or on an attached Additional Page.

Step 4: Expenses. Enter the requested information.

Step 5: Other party's income. Make your best estimate based on information and documents you have. It is important to try to get the best documentation possible to support your estimate.

Step 6: Date and sign. Enter date of your signature, type in your name on the line on the left, and check the box "Petitioner" under your signature line.

Page total. Enter total number of forms filed in this set—"4" if you are requesting child support, otherwise "3."

Figure 16C-1: Income and Expense Declaration

Ⓐ   Ⓑ   Ⓒ   Ⓗ

ATTORNEY OR PARTY WITHOUT ATTORNEY *(Name and Address):*	TELEPHONE NO.: (805) 427-9326	FOR COURT USE ONLY

CATHERINE J. LYNCH,
AKA KATE LYNCH
6625 SUENO APT. B
SANTA BARBARA, CALIFORNIA 93103

Ⓓ
ATTORNEY FOR *(Name):* CATHERINE J. LYNCH

SUPERIOR COURT OF CALIFORNIA, COUNTY OF SANTA BARBARA
STREET ADDRESS: 1100 ANACAPA STREET

Ⓔ
MAILING ADDRESS: SANTA BARBARA, CALIFORNIA 93103
CITY AND ZIP CODE:
BRANCH NAME:

Ⓕ
PETITIONER/PLAINTIFF: CATHERINE J. LYNCH

RESPONDENT/DEFENDANT: SHAWN F. GALLAGHER

Ⓖ

INCOME AND EXPENSE DECLARATION	CASE NUMBER: 323404

Step 1 Attachments to this summary	I have completed [X] Income [X] Expense [X] Child Support Information forms. *(If child support is not an issue, do not complete the Child Support Information Form. If your only income is AFDC, do not complete the Income Information Form.)*

Step 2 Answer all questions that apply to you	1. Are you receiving or have you applied for or do you intend to apply for welfare or AFDC? ☐ Receiving ☐ Applied for ☐ Intend to apply for [X] No
	 2. What is your date of birth *(month/day/year)*? 05-28-65
	 3. What is your occupation? BARTENDER
	 4. Highest year of education completed: 12
	 5. Are you currently employed? [X] Yes ☐ No
	     a. If yes: (1) Where do you work? *(name and address):* GRANDMA GERTIES 345 DEL NORTE, SANTA BARBARA, CA
	            (2) When did you start work there *(month/year)*? 03/94
	     b. If no: (1) When did you last work *(month/year)*? ....
	            (2) What were your gross monthly earnings? ....
	 6. What is the total number of minor children you are legally obligated to support? 1

Step 3 Monthly income Information	7. Net monthly disposable income *(from line 16a of Income Information)*: .... $ 811.00 8. Current net monthly disposable income *(if different from line 7, explain below or on Attachment 8)*: $
Step 4 Expense Information	9. Total monthly expenses from line 2q of Expense Information: .... $ 2,154.00 10. Amount of these expenses paid by others: .... $
Step 5 Other party's income	11. My estimate of the other party's gross monthly income is: .... $ 2154.00
Step 6 Date and sign this form	I declare under penalty of perjury under the laws of the State of California that the foregoing and the attached information forms are true and correct. Date: AUGUST 3, 1995 ▶ CATHERINE J. LYNCH *(TYPE OR PRINT NAME)* *(SIGNATURE OF DECLARANT)* [X] Petitioner ☐ Respondent Page one of 4

Form Adopted by Rule 1285.50
Judicial Council of California
1285.50 (Rev. January 1, 1995)

INCOME AND EXPENSE DECLARATION
(Family Law)

Figure 16C-2: Income Information

(A) Short caption. Type in the names of the parties, exactly as entered in the other captions, but omit any aliases. On the third line of the caption, enter your name again to show this is *your* income information.

(1) Total gross wages. All money you received through employment, including tips, commissions, bonuses and overtime—over the past 12 months. Give the gross amount before any deductions are taken for anything—the largest number on the paystub or W-2 form, not the amount received when you cased the paychecks.

(2) All other money received during the past 12 months, not including welfare, SSI, any child support, or spousal support from the abuser. Read the list of included funds to help jog your memory. Attach income and expense detail sheet for each business or rental activity. Enter amounts from each source on lines 2a–d and continue on an Additional Page if you need more lines.

(3) Total income. Total of lines 1–2d.

For items (14–16), you will enter the monthly average (the total over the last 12 months divided by 12) *and* the current actual figure for the last month.

(4) Gross monthly income. Item (4a) is item (3) divided by 12.

Deductions from income. Items (5–11) can be found on your pay stubs, tax returns, or reports from your accountant.

Item (7): Social Security. If you are self-employed, you can include amounts paid for equivalent coverage.

Item (8): Health insurance. Do not include amounts to cover anyone but you and your children.

Items (10) and (11): Mandatory union dues and retirement. Do not include amounts that are voluntary; include only amounts that are deducted as a condition of employment. Do not include amounts already included in item (7).

Item (12): Support paid. Include only support paid to a child or spouse according to a court order. Support paid voluntarily to a child (not according to a court order) not listed in this proceeding can be included.

Item (13): Job-related expenses: expenses required by the employer, such as tools, special clothing, or travel for the job, but only if not reimbursed by the employer. Amounts included here must be described and explained on an Additional Page.

Items (18) to (21): Assets. Enter whatever amounts you may have in any of the listed categories. For item (21), estimate the fair market value for your real and personal property—the amount you could clear if you were to sell it all now and pay off loans due on the same items. Type in a very general description of what the figure refers to: "Auto, household goods, real estate."

Page total. This will be page 2 of either 3 or 4—"4" if you are requesting child support, otherwise "3."

Pay stubs: If you are paid wages, attach a copy of your three most recent pay stubs.

Figure 16C-2: Income Information

PETITIONER/PLAINTIFF: CATHERINE J. LYNCH	CASE NUMBER:
RESPONDENT/DEFENDANT: SHAWN F. GALLAGHER	
INCOME INFORMATION OF (name): CATHERINE J. LYNCH	323404

1. Total gross salary or wages, including commissions, bonuses, and overtime paid during the last 12 months: 1. $ <u>12,000.00</u>
2. All other money received during the last 12 months except welfare, AFDC,   *Specify sources below:*
   SSI, spousal support from this marriage, or any child support.   2a. $ _____
   Include pensions, social security, disability, unemployment, military basic allowance for quarters (BAQ), spousal support from a different marriage, dividends, interest or royalty, trust income, and annuities.   2b. $ _____
   Include income from a business, rental properties, and reimbursement of job-related expenses.   2c. $ _____
       Prepare and attach a schedule showing gross receipts less cash expenses for each business or rental property.   2d. $ _____
3. Add lines 1 through 2d . . . .   3. $ <u>12,000.00</u>
   Divide line 3 by 12 and place result on line 4a.

	Average last 12 months:	Last month:
4. Gross income	4a. $ <u>1,000.00</u>	4b. $ <u>1,000.00</u>
5. State income tax	5a. $ <u>12.00</u>	5b. $ <u>12.00</u>
6. Federal income tax	6a. $ <u>66.00</u>	6b. $ <u>66.00</u>
7. Social Security and Hospital Tax ("FICA" and "MEDI") or self-employment tax, or the amount used to secure retirement or disability benefits	7a. $ <u>111.00</u>	7b. $ <u>111.00</u>
8. Health insurance for you and any children you are required to support	8a. $ _____	8b. $ _____
9. State disability insurance	9a. $ _____	9b. $ _____
10. Mandatory union dues	10a. $ _____	10b. $ _____
11. Mandatory retirement and pension fund contributions . . . . *Do not include any deduction claimed in item 7.*	11a. $ _____	11b. $ _____
12. Court-ordered child support, court-ordered spousal support, and voluntarily paid child support in an amount not more than the guideline amount, **actually being paid for a relationship *other* than that involved in this proceeding:**	12a. $ _____	12b. $ _____
13. Necessary job-related expenses *(attach explanation)*	13a. $ _____	13b. $ _____
14. Hardship deduction (Line 4d on Child Support Information Form)	14a. $ _____	14b. $ _____
15. Add lines 5 through 14 . . . . Total monthly deductions:	15a. $ <u>189.00</u>	15b. $ <u>189.00</u>
16. Subtract line 15 from line 4 . . . . Net monthly disposable income:	16a. $ <u>811.00</u>	16b. $ <u>811.00</u>

17. AFDC, welfare, spousal support from this marriage, and child support from other relationships received each month: . . . .   17. $ _____
18. Cash and checking accounts: . . . .   18. $ <u>150.00</u>
19. Savings, credit union, certificates of deposit, and money market accounts: . . . .   19. $ <u>20.00</u>
20. Stocks, bonds, and other liquid assets: . . . .   20. $ _____
21. All other property, real or personal *(specify below):* . . . .   21. $ <u>3,500.00</u>

Attach a copy of your three most recent pay stubs.   Page <u>2</u> of <u>4</u>

Form Adopted by Rule 1285.50a
Judicial Council of California   **INCOME INFORMATION**
1285.50a (Rev. January 1, 1995)   (Family Law)

Figure 16C-3: Expense Information

(A) Short caption. Type in the names of the parties, exactly as entered in the other captions, but omit any aliases. On the third line of the caption, enter your name again to show this is *your* expense information.

(1) People living with you.

(1a) List all persons living with you whose expenses are included with yours. Give the name, age, relationship to you and gross monthly income of each person listed. If there are more than 4, check the box and continue on an Additional Page.

(1b) List all other persons living with you who are not listed above. Give their name, age, relationship to you and their gross monthly income. If there are more than 4, check the box and continue on an Additional Page.

(2) Monthly expenses. Enter your monthly expenses, using an average over the past 12 months for expenses that vary. Add up the total and enter it at item (2q). Do not try to make expenses match income. List reasonable minimum expenses, even if you haven't been able to afford them. Identify items that are projected or estimated. Do not leave out amounts for haircuts, gifts, travel, newspapers, books, cosmetics, childrens games and toys, and so on.

(3) Debts. List your debts. For each item, enter what the debt is for, the monthly payment, balance due, and the date of your last payment. If you need more room, check the box and continue on an Additional Page.

(4) Attorney fees. Type "In Pro Per" on the signature line for the attorney.

Page total. This will be page 3 of either 3 or 4—"4" if you are requesting child support, otherwise "3."

Figure 16C-4: Child Support Information

This form is required only if you are requesting an order for child support.

(A) Short caption. Type in the names of the parties, exactly as entered in the other captions, but omit any aliases. On the third line of the caption, enter your name again to show this is *your* expense information.

(1) Health insurance for your children. Indicate whether it is or is not available through your employment.

(1a) If you have health insurance for children who are listed in this action, give the monthly amount paid by you or for you, but not amounts paid by the employer.

(1b–d) Give details about the health insurance carrier.

(2) Child care timeshare. Estimate the percentage of time you and Respondent have primary physical care of the listed children. If your schedule is different for different children, enter the average. Type in "Average" then type in the different timeshares for the children. For example: Respondent has Billy 30% of the time and Sue for 15%.

Figure 16C-3: Expense Information

Ⓐ

PETITIONER/PLAINTIFF: CATHERINE J. LYNCH				CASE NUMBER:
RESPONDENT/DEFENDANT: SHAWN F. GALLAGHER				323404
EXPENSE INFORMATION OF (name): CATHERINE J. LYNCH				

1.

a. List all persons living in your home whose expenses are included below and their income:
☐ Continued on Attachment 1a.

	name	age	relationship	gross monthly income
1.	RALPH	5	SON	0
2.				
3.				
4.				

b. List all other persons living in your home and their income:
☐ Continued on Attachment 1b.

1.				
2.				
3.				

2. MONTHLY EXPENSES

a. Residence payments
  (1) [X] Rent or ☐ mortgage .... $ __750.00__

  (2) If mortgage, include:
    Average principle...... $ _____

    Average interest....... $ _____
    Impound for real
      property taxes...... $ _____
    Impound for home-
      owner's insurance ... $ _____

  (3) Real property taxes (if not
    included in item (2))................. $ _____

  (4) Homeowner's or renter's insurance
    (if not included in item (2)) .... $ _____

  (5) Maintenance .... $ __10.00__

b. Unreimbursed medical and dental
  expenses.............................. $ _____

c. Child care............................... $ __250.00__

d. Children's education .... $ __200.00__

e. Food at home and household supplies .. $ __400.00__

f. Food eating out .... $ __60.00__

g. Utilities............................... $ __85.00__

h. Telephone .... $ __45.00__

i. Laundry and cleaning.................. $ __50.00__

j. Clothing............................. $ __50.00__

k. Insurance (life, accident, etc. Do not include auto, home, or health insurance) $ _____

l. Education (specify): CITY .... $ __90.00__
  COLLEGE

m. Entertainment....................... $ __14.00__

n. Transportation and auto expenses
  (insurance, gas, oil, repair)........... $ __150.00__

o. Installment payments (insert total and
  itemize below in item 3) .... $ _____

p. Other (specify):...................... $ _____

q. TOTAL EXPENSES (a-p)............... $ __2,154.00__
  (do not include amounts in a(2))

3. ITEMIZATION OF INSTALLMENT PAYMENTS OR OTHER DEBTS ☐ Continued on Attachment 3.

CREDITOR'S NAME	PAYMENT FOR	MONTHLY PAYMENT	BALANCE	DATE LAST PAYMENT MADE

4. ATTORNEY FEES

a. To date I have paid my attorney for fees and costs: $ [_____] The source of this money was:

b. I owe to date the following fees and costs over the amount paid:

c. My arrangement for attorney fees and costs is:

I confirm this information and fee arrangement. ▶

_____
(SIGNATURE OF ATTORNEY)

IN PRO PER
_____
(TYPE OR PRINT NAME OF ATTORNEY)

Page __3__ of __4__

Form Adopted by Rule 1285.50b
Judicial Council of California
1285.50b (Rev. January 1, 1995)

EXPENSE INFORMATION
(Family Law)

Figure 16C-4: Child Support Information

PETITIONER/PLAINTIFF: CATHERINE J. LYNCH RESPONDENT/DEFENDANT: SHAWN F. GALLAGHER CHILD SUPPORT INFORMATION OF *(name):* CATHERINE J. LYNCH	CASE NUMBER: 323404

THIS PAGE MUST BE COMPLETED IF CHILD SUPPORT IS AN ISSUE.

1. Health insurance for my children ☐ is ☒ is not available through my employer.
   a. Monthly cost paid by me or on my behalf for the children *only* is: $ _____
      Do not include the amount paid or payable by your employer.
   b. Name of carrier:
   c. Address of carrier:

   d. Policy or group policy number:

2. Approximate percentage of time each parent has primary physical responsibility for the children:
   Mother 90 % Father 10 %

3. ☒ The court is requested to order the following as additional child support:
   a. ☒ Child care costs related to employment or to reasonably necessary education or training for employment skills
      (1) Monthly amount currently paid by mother: $ 250.00
      (2) Monthly amount currently paid by father: $
   b. ☐ Uninsured health care costs for the children *(for each cost state the purpose for which the cost was incurred and the estimated monthly, yearly, or lump sum amount paid by each parent):*

   c. ☒ Educational or other special needs of the children *(for each cost state the purpose for which the cost was incurred and the estimated monthly, yearly, or lump sum amount paid by each parent):*
      $200.00 PAID FOR RALPH'S PRESCHOOL; 100% PAID BY CATHERINE LYNCH.

   d. ☐ Travel expense for visitation
      (1) Monthly amount currently paid by mother: $
      (2) Monthly amount currently paid by father: $

4. ☐ The court is requested to allow the deductions identified below, which are justifiable expenses that have caused an extreme financial hardship.

	Amount paid per month	How many months will you need to make these payments
a. ☐ Extraordinary health care expense *(specify and attach any supporting documents):*	$_____	_____
b. ☐ Uninsured catastrophic losses *(specify and attach supporting documents):*	$_____	_____
c. ☐ Minimum basic living expenses of dependent minor children from other marriages or relationships who live with you *(specify names and ages of these children):*	$_____	_____
d. Total hardship deductions requested *(add lines a - c):*	$_____	

Page 4 of 4

Form Adopted by Rule 1285.50c
Judicial Council of California
1285.50c [Rev. January 1, 1995]

CHILD SUPPORT INFORMATION
(Family Law)

(3) Additional child care costs. In addition to basic child support, you can request that Respondent pay his share of certain additional child care costs. Check this box if you are requesting additional child support for any of the following:

(3a) Child care. Check this box if you or Respondent pay for child care to enable you to work or get education or training for employment skills.

(3b) Uninsured health care. Check this box if the children have health care expenses not covered by insurance. Describe each cost and give the amount.

(3c) Education and special needs. Check this box if you have expenses for educational or special needs of the children. Describe each expense and give the amount.

(3d) Travel expenses for visitation. Check this box if you or Respondent face special expenses to visit with the children. Describe each expense and give the amount.

(4) Hardship expenses. Check this box if you face any of the listed hardship expenses and want them to be allowed by the court. Provide the requested information and enter the total at item 4d and also at line 14 on the Income Information sheet.

Page total. This will be page 4 of 4.

D. Wage and Earnings Assignment Order

If you request an order for child support, you have to file this form, whether or not Respondent is employed at this time.

Caption. Complete items A–H exactly as you did on the Application. Check the box for "Child Support."

Identify Respondent. On the line immediately below the heading, enter Respondent's name and birth date.

(1a) Check this box.

(2) Enter the name and address of the recipient. If you are on welfare, or if the children are receiving AFDC, or if you choose to have payments made through the court, enter the name and address of the court officer designated to receive support payments for your county. Ask the clerk for this information.

Problem payers: If you don't know where your spouse or your spouse's employer is located, take your Restraining Order After Hearing and Wage Assignment Order to your DA's office. They are required to conduct a parent locator search and notify the court of the results. If your spouse is often unemployed or frequently changes jobs or might otherwise be difficult to chase down for support payments, consider having all support paid through the court officer designated in your county to receive support payments and let them administer the collection of support. Find out from the clerk who does this job in your county, then go down and talk to them about how their service works. Get a sense for whether you would rather have them do it or do it yourself.

Figure 16D: Wage and Earnings Assignment Order

Ⓐ   Ⓑ   Ⓒ   Ⓗ

Ⓓ   Ⓔ   Ⓕ   Ⓖ

ATTORNEY OR PARTY WITHOUT ATTORNEY *(Name and Address):*   TELEPHONE NO.: (805) 427-9326

CATHERINE J. LYNCH,
AKA KATE LYNCH
6625 SUENO APT. B
SANTA BARBARA, CALIFORNIA 93103

ATTORNEY FOR *(Name):* IN PRO PER

SUPERIOR COURT OF CALIFORNIA, COUNTY OF SANTA BARBARA
STREET ADDRESS: 1100 ANACAPA STREET
MAILING ADDRESS: SANTA BARBARA, CALIFORNIA 93103
CITY AND ZIP CODE:
BRANCH NAME:

PETITIONER/PLAINTIFF: CATHERINE J. LYNCH

RESPONDENT/DEFENDANT: SHAWN F. GALLAGHER

FOR COURT USE ONLY

WAGE AND EARNINGS ASSIGNMENT ORDER
☐ Modification ☒ Child Support ☐ Spousal or Family Support

CASE NUMBER: 323404

TO THE PAYOR: This is a court order. You must withhold a portion of the earnings of *(obligor's name and date of birth):*
SHAWN F. GALLAGHER 11-07-62
and pay as directed below. *(An explanation of this order is printed on the reverse.)*

THE COURT ORDERS YOU TO
1. Pay part of the earnings of the employee or other person ordered to pay support as follows:
   a. ☒ $ per month current **child support.**   d. ☐ $ per month **child support arrearages.**
   b. ☐ $ per month current **spousal support.**   e. ☐ $ per month **spousal support arrearages.**
   c. ☐ $ per month current **family support.**   f. ☐ $ per month **family support arrearages.**
   g. Total deductions per month: $

2. ☒ The payments ordered under items 1a, 1b, and 1c shall be paid to *(name, address):* CATHERINE J. LYNCH
   6625 SUENO APT. B, SANTA BARBARA, CA 93103

3. ☐ The payments ordered under item 1d, 1e, and 1f shall be paid to *(name, address):*

4. The payments ordered under item 1 shall continue until further written notice from payee or the court.

5. ☐ This order modifies an existing order. The amount you must withhold may have changed. The existing order continues in effect until this modification is effective.
6. This order affects all earnings payable beginning as soon as possible but not later than 10 days after you receive it.
7. Give the obligor a copy of this order within 10 days.
8. ☐ Other *(specify):*

For the purposes of this order, the arrearages are set as follows:
       Amount   As of *(date)*
9. a. ☐ Child support:
   b. ☐ Spousal support:
   c. ☐ Family support:

Date: _____
     JUDGE OF THE SUPERIOR COURT

(See reverse for information and instructions)

Form Adopted by Rule 1285.70
Judicial Council of California
1285.70 [Rev. January 1, 1995]

WAGE AND EARNINGS ASSIGNMENT ORDER
(Family Law - Domestic Violence Prevention - Uniform Parentage)

Family Code, § 5208
Code of Civil Procedure, § 706.031
15 U.S.C. §§ 1672-1673

Changes: The paying spouse must notify the recipient of changes in employment within 10 days and give the name and address of the new employer (Family Code §5281). If the paying spouse terminates employment, the employer must notify the recipient by mail on or before the date the next payment would be due (Family Code §5282). The recipient must notify the employer of changes in address if being paid directly, or notify the designated court officer if payments are being made through the court. If payments are undeliverable for six months because the recipient failed to provide a current address, the employer or court officer will stop making payments and refund all undelivered money to the paying spouse.

E. Declaration

This form is used whenever you want to file statements from witnesses or additional information from yourself. It is also used for the Declaration Re Ex Parte Notice, as described in Chapter 15D. Always keep a blank of this form on hand, as it may have several uses.

It better to type this form, but if circumstances require it, the form can be completed in black ballpoint pen. Print, and make it as clear as possible.

For clarification, the Declaration is used for independent statements not being made part of a form. The Additional Page is used whenever you have information that won't fit in the space available on some particular form.

Figure 16E: Declaration

Caption. Complete items A–H exactly as you did on the Application. Add the case number, if you have already been given one.

Header. Under the caption box, in capitals, type "DECLARATION OF" and add the name of the person making the declaration.

Statement. Enter the statement of the witness. Be concise and stick to facts, as discussed in Chapter 14. Make it all fit on the one page.

Date and sign. Enter date of signing, type in the name of the person signing on the line to the left of the signature line, and check a box below the signature line. For a witness, check "Other" and enter "Witness;" check "Petitioner" if it is your own Declaration.

Figure 16E: Declaration

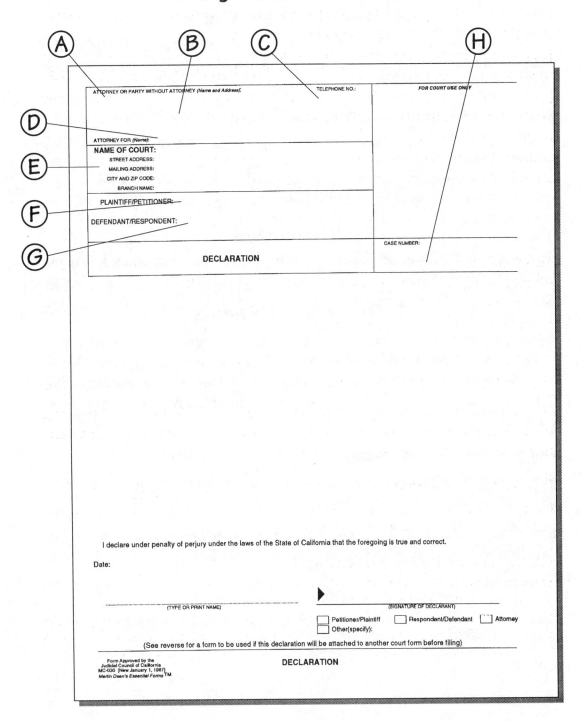

F. Application for Reissuance of Order to Show Cause

If you do not get Respondent served in the time set by the court before the hearing, you should file this form and go back to the judge for a new hearing date and renewal of your temporary restraining orders.

Figure 16F: Application for Reissuance of OSC

Caption. Complete items A–G exactly as you did on the Application. Add your case number at item H.

(2) Reason for reissuance. Check a box to show why you need a reissuance.

(a) Couldn't serve Respondent on time (the one you will almost always use).

(b) Need time to complete required mediation.

(c) Other (describe reason):

Date and sign. Enter date of your signature and type in your name on the line to the left of your signature line.

G. Order Attachments

Optionally, and for your convenience, these forms can be used to help you make out your orders. You can borrow language from these forms and use it in your own orders, or you can simply attach any of these forms to either the Temporary Restraining Order (Chapter 15B) or the Order After Hearing (Chapter 15C).

Figures 16G (1-3): Order Attachment forms

First is an official judicial council form; the other two are adapted from forms used in Los Angeles.

Simply complete the heading, check the appropriate boxes, complete any orders that require more information, and attach the form(s).

Figure 16F: Application for Reissuance of Order To Show Cause

Ⓐ Ⓑ Ⓒ Ⓗ

Ⓓ Ⓔ Ⓕ Ⓖ

ATTORNEY OR PARTY WITHOUT ATTORNEY (Name and Address):   TELEPHONE NO: (805) 427-9326

CATHERINE J. LYNCH,
AKA KATE LYNCH
6625 SUENO APT. B
SANTA BARBARA, CALIFORNIA 93103
ATTORNEY FOR (Name): IN PRO PER

FOR COURT USE ONLY

SUPERIOR COURT OF CALIFORNIA, COUNTY OF SANTA BARBARA

STREET ADDRESS: 1100 ANACAPA STREET
MAILING ADDRESS: SANTA BARBARA, CALIFORNIA 93103
CITY AND ZIP CODE:
BRANCH NAME:

PLAINTIFF: CATHERINE J. LYNCH

DEFENDANT: SHAWN F. GALLAGHER

APPLICATION AND ORDER FOR REISSUANCE OF ORDER TO SHOW CAUSE
(Family Law — Domestic Violence Prevention — Uniform Parentage)

CASE NUMBER:
323404

1. Plaintiff requests the court to reissue the Order To Show Cause and Temporary Restraining Order originally issued as follows:
   a. Order To Show Cause was issued on (date):
   b. Order To Show Cause was last set for hearing on (date):
   c. Order To Show Cause has been reissued previously (number of times):
2. Plaintiff requests reissuance of the order because:
   a. ☒ Defendant was unable to be served as required before the hearing date.
   b. ☐ The hearing was continued because the parties were referred to court mediators, conciliation court, or family court services.
   c. ☐ Other (Specify):

   I declare under penalty of perjury under the laws of the State of California that the foregoing is true and correct.
   Date:

   CATHERINE J. LYNCH .... _____
   (TYPE OR PRINT NAME)   (SIGNATURE)

   ORDER

3. IT IS ORDERED that the Order To Show Cause issued as shown in item 1 above is re-issued and reset for hearing in this court as follows:

Date:	time:	dept.:	rm.:

   at the street address of the court shown above.

   b. By the close of business on the date of this order a copy of this order and any proof of service shall be given to the law enforcement agencies named in the Order To Show Cause as follows:
   ☐ the plaintiff shall deliver.
   ☐ the plaintiff's attorney shall deliver.
   ☐ the clerk of the court shall mail.
   c. A copy of this order shall be attached to documents to be served on the defendant, as directed in the Order to Show Cause, and shall also be served on the defendant.
   d. All other orders contained in the Order To Show cause remain in full force and effect unless modified by this order. THE ORDER TO SHOW CAUSE AND THIS ORDER EXPIRE ON THE DATE AND TIME OF THE HEARING SHOWN IN THE BOX ABOVE UNLESS EXTENDED BY THE COURT.

   ►

   DATE: JUDGE OF THE SUPERIOR COURT

   CLERK'S CERTIFICATE OF MAILING
   I certify that I am not a party to this cause and that a copy of the foregoing was mailed first class, postage prepaid, in a sealed envelope addressed as shown in the Order To Show Cause and that the foregoing was mailed and this certificate was executed at

   (place): .... , California,

   on (date):   Clerk, by _____ , Deputy

Form Adopted by Rule 1296.15
Judicial Council of California
1296.15 (Rev. January 1, 1985)
1296.15

APPLICATION AND ORDER FOR REISSUANCE
OF ORDER TO SHOW CAUSE
(Family Law — Domestic Violence Prevention — Uniform Parentage)

76A509—RD057—1-85
CCP 527(b)

Figure 16G-1: Order Attachment 1

PLAINTIFF *(Name)*:

DEFENDANT *(Name)*:

CASE NUMBER:

DOMESTIC VIOLENCE MISCELLANEOUS ORDERS ATTACHMENT
(Attachment to Findings and Order After Hearing (rule 1296.31)
- or -
to Restraining Order After Hearing (CLETS) (rule 1296.29))

1. a. ☐ Plaintiff is given exclusive use, possession, and control of the following property:

   b. ☐ Defendant shall make the following payments coming due while this order is in effect:
Debt	Payable to	Amount of payment	Date payable
		$	

2. ☐ Defendant shall pay the following attorney fees and costs:
	Payable to	Amount of payment	Date payable
		$	

3. ☐ Defendant shall make the following payments as restitution:
	Payable to	Amount of payment	Date payable
		$	

4. a. ☐ The following parties shall participate in counseling as the court directs: ☐ Plaintiff ☐ Defendant
   b. ☐ Defendant shall participate in counseling for batterers.

5. ☐ OTHER ORDERS:

If there are minor children of this relationship, obtain an order for child support.
Use the Child Support Order Attachment (Form 1296.31B) or item 5, other orders, on this form

Page _____ of _____

Form Adopted by Rule 1296.31E
Judicial Council of California
1296.31E [Rev. January 1, 1995]

DOMESTIC VIOLENCE MISCELLANEOUS ORDERS ATTACHMENT
(Domestic Violence Prevention - Uniform Parentage Act)

Family Code §§ 6324, 6340-6344

CEB

Figure 16G-2: Order Attachment 2

PETITIONER *(Name):*	CASE NUMBER:
RESPONDENT *(Name):*	

ATTACHMENT ☐ A ☐ B ☐ __ to the
☐ **Order To Show Cause and Temporary Restraining Order**
☐ **Restraining Order After Hearing**

ORDERS RELATING TO CHILDREN:

☐ Neither party shall remove the minor child(ren) from the State of California without the prior written consent of the other party or an order of the court.

☐ Parties must make and keep at least one appointment in Conciliation Court prior to the OSC hearing.

☐ Police shall serve and enforce all TRO's, including but not limited to, escorting Petitioner to Respondent's residence, retrieving the parties' minor child(ren) from the Respondent, and returning the parties' minor child(ren) to Petitioner.

☐ Respondent shall return to Petitioner their minor child(ren) forthwith.

☐ No visitation pending the OSC hearing.

☐ Respondent may have the following visitation pending the OSC hearing:

☐ The Respondent may not use alcohol or drugs within 72 hours of, or during, visitation.

☐ The Respondent may not drive the child(ren) while under the influence of alcohol or drugs.

☐ Neutral pick-up and drop-off location for any visitation (specify location):

ORDER FOR DWELLING EXCLUSION:

☐ Police shall enforce and serve all temporary restraining orders, including but not limited to, escorting Petitioner to the residence, serving Respondent with the TRO and escorting Respondent away from the residence.

☐ Police shall serve and enforce all TRO's.

Number of orders checked above: ___

Dated: _____   _____
                                   Judge of the Superior Court

Figure 16G-3: Order Attachment 3

PETITIONER *(Name):*

RESPONDENT *(Name):*

CASE NUMBER:

ATTACHMENT ☐ A ☐ B ☐ ___ to the
☐ Order To Show Cause and Temporary Restraining Order
☐ Restraining Order After Hearing

ORDERS RELATING TO PROPERTY OF MARRIED PARTIES:

☐ The Respondent shall be restrained from transferring, encumbering, hypothecating, concealing, or in any way disposing of any property, real or personal, whether community, quasi-community, or separate, except in the usual course of business or for the necessities of life. Applicant shall be notified at least five business days before any proposed extraordinary expenditures and an accounting of such be made to the court.

☐ Both parties are restrained and enjoined from cashing, borrowing against, canceling, transferring, disposing of, or changing the beneficiaries of any insurance or other coverage including life, health, automobile, and disability held for the benefit of the parties or their minor child(ren).

☐ Neither party shall incur any debts or liabilities for which the other party may be held responsible, other than in the ordinary course of business or for the necessities of life.

OTHER ORDERS:

☐ Police shall serve and enforce all TRO's.

☐ Petitioner shall be allowed access to Respondent's residence to retrieve his/her (and/or child(ren)'s) personal belongings with a police escort and until Petitioner has retrieved all such belongings from Respondent's residence.

☐ If the Respondent is served with the TRO at the residence, he/she shall retrieve his/her personal belongings at that time and shall return to Petitioner all keys and copies of keys to the residence. However, if the Respondent is not served with the TRO at the residence, Respondent shall have access to the residence of the Petitioner only once and only with a police escort to retrieve his/her personal belongings, if any, and to return to Petitioner all keys and copies of keys to the residence. The Respondent may otherwise mail the keys to the Petitioner, or give them to a neutral party to return to the Petitioner.

☐ Respondent shall return to Petitioner forthwith Petitioner's (describe):

Number of orders checked above: ___

Dated: _____   _____
                                          Judge of the Superior Court

Chapter 17

Filing the forms—
your first trip to court

Things to know before you go

When and where?

Some courts will have you file your papers at the filing desk (or window) in the clerk's office, while others will have you go directly to the courtroom and file there. If you haven't already done it, call the superior court clerk and ask:

✦ Where do I file my application for a domestic violence restraining order?

✦ Can you tell me how to get to the courthouse and the filing window?

✦ Which courtroom hears applications for an ex parte DVRO?

✦ At what time do they here these cases?

✦ How do I get to the courtroom?

✦ What is the phone number of that courtroom?

✦ Does the court take live testimony from witnesses or consider only their declarations? *You may have to call the clerk in the courtroom for this one.*

✦ How much notice to Respondent is required in this county before an ex parte hearing (your first trip to the courtroom)?

Dress and attitude

When you go to the courthouse to do business, it *does* matter how you dress and how you act. Don't go out and buy anything special, just do your best with what you've got. Dress in clean, pressed, conservative, comfortable clothes. Wear something you would wear to apply for a bank loan—dark tones, small prints, solid colors with little jewelry or makeup. Wear comfortable shoes (polished, if they are leather) because you may be making several trips back and forth between the clerk's office and the courtroom.

Always act calm and businesslike. Drama disturbs people. Upsetting things may have happened to you, but they are not happening in the courtroom or to the courthouse staff. You will get along much better if you can stay calm and focused on the business at hand.

Get someone to watch your children. Children don't do well in courtrooms and few courts have day care facilities. Many judges won't allow them in the courtroom at all. You don't need the distraction and stress of keeping your kids under control. Don't bring them.

About clerks

You may find a clerk who is gracious and patient, even friendly. Then again, you may not. If you happen to run into a clerk who is unpleasant, try to remember that clerks are typically overworked, underpaid and under stress from a caseload beyond reason. If your clerk is difficult or even hostile, stay polite no matter how badly they may act. Don't take anything personally; lawyers get the same treatment. If necessary, ask for another clerk to help you, ask for a supervisor, or leave and come back later. Under no circumstances should you *ever* respond in kind or with anything other than calm politeness. This is especially true of the clerk and bailiff in the courtroom—the judge's personal staff. Never, never, never antagonize the judge's staff.

Check your papers

If you have time to do it, you'll feel more confident if you have someone experienced look at your papers before you go to the courthouse. Take your completed forms to your shelter, counselor, or a domestic violence legal clinic and have them checked. Some courts require that your papers be checked by their in-house clinic. If so, be prepared to make corrections at the courthouse. Take two or three blank Declaration forms, extra paper, correction fluid, and an extra set of blank forms with you.

Be organized

You will earn big points at the courthouse if you know which forms are which and hand the clerks what they ask for without shuffling through a big pile of loose papers in a confused manner. Keep your papers in order; bring at least two copies of each form and keep them with the originals. Make a checklist of the forms you are filing, so if the forms do get mixed up you can get them back in order again.

Giving notice to Respondent

When you first go in to file your papers, you can ask for immediate temporary orders against Respondent. If you are going to ask for such orders, you have to give the abuser notice unless you have a good reason not to.

When you get the phone number of the court that hears DVROs, call the clerk in that courtroom and confirm the notice requirements for your county. Ask for an example, to be perfectly clear. If the clerk says 24 hours is required, this may mean that the notice is to be given by 12 noon the day before the hearing which will be held at 1:30 pm. In Los Angeles, six business hours is required. This is defined as notice by 11:00 am the day before the hearing which would be at 8:30 am the next day. In other courts four hours is required, but the court still requires notice by 12 noon the day before the hearing at 8:30 am the next day. So ask. Many attorneys give two days' notice to be safe. If you are out of the house in a shelter, and safe, notice can be given unless there are other circumstances which make notice to Respondent unwise.

If it is safe to give notice: Call him or have a friend call him the day before you go to court. Tell him you are getting a restraining order. Tell him the date, time and place where you will apply for these orders. Give him the address of the court and the courtroom number. In Los Angeles, for example, he must have at least six business hours notice, so call him by 11 am the day before. After giving notice, complete the Declaration Re Ex Parte Notice and indicate when notice was given, what was said, and who did it. The person who did it signs the form.

If you are afraid to give notice or can't do it: If you can state reasons why you are afraid of what he will do if he finds out you are going to court, or if you tried very hard to do so and couldn't find him, then explain this to the court in the Declaration Re Ex Parte Notice form.

The Declaration Re Ex Parte Notice (Chapter 15D) is where you tell the court when and how notice was given to Respondent, or explain why notice was not given or could not be given.

What to do at the courthouse

File your papers

Go to the courthouse early, so you have extra time in case you have trouble finding your way, or in case there's a line ahead of you, or in case there's a security check. In some courthouses, you have to pass through a metal detector and send your handbags through an X-ray machine. Of course, you should not bring weapons of any kind to the courthouse.

The first thing you do is file your papers. Depending on the court, you will either do this at the clerk's office or at the courtroom where your case will be heard. You have already called ahead to ask how this works in your county. If your papers are filed first at the clerk's office, you will next be directed to the courtroom with your file. Go to the courtroom and present the file to the court clerk.

In the courtroom

This first trip to court is called the *ex parte* hearing. Take two or three blank Declaration forms, a blank set of all the forms, a black ballpoint pen, and correction fluid with you.

Check in with the court clerk or the bailiff; they'll direct you. You may also be asked to log in by writing the date and time with your name in a ledger book. Cases are taken in the order logged. This is important, so be sure you log in if that's the system.

Hand your paperwork to the clerk. The first thing they will look at is your Declaration Re Ex Parte Notice. If you are asking for temporary orders at this time, the clerk needs to see that notice was given or, if not, why not. The clerk wants to know if Respondent might show up in court.

The Respondent will not be there if he has not been given notice. The clerk will look at your Declaration Re Ex Parte Notice to see if your reason for not giving notice is sufficient. If Respondent *was* given notice, the clerk will ask you if Respondent has arrived. If not, you may be asked whether you know if he is coming. Just tell what you know for a fact. Either way, the judge may wait until "second call" before acting on your Application.

If you think Respondent might show up, make sure you have one complete set of papers for Respondent (see Chapter 18) and bring a support person with you who can hand them to him and later sign a Proof of Service. Make sure Respondent's set includes a blank Responsive Declaration. If you are requesting child support, also include blank Income and Expense Declaration forms.

If Respondent *does* show up in court, the judge will order him to appear at the hearing and the clerk will make a note of this on the record. This is called a "minute order." This means you do not have to serve him (Chapter 18). Before you leave the courtroom, be sure to ask the clerk for a copy of the minute order for your records.

Submit papers to the judge. Next the clerk will look at your Order to Show Cause, Temporary Restraining Order and Application and Declarations. These papers will be submitted to the judge.

> Local form? Make sure you also submit a Certificate of Assignment if required in your county, and Proposed Order attachments if you are seeking additional orders. It is essential that a complete Order be already prepared.

At this point, be prepared to do some waiting. Your case might be heard right away; you might win the lottery, too. Attorneys believe that the less prepared they are the more likely the judge is to call them first. Don't try it. Instead, bring a good book to read while you wait. Sit in the back behind other people and be very inconspicuous if you decide to read in the courtroom.

If you have children with the abuser, tell the clerk you want to ask the judge if you are required to go through conciliation or mediation before the hearing. If so, ask for details and instructions, then go home and read Appendix B.

Get Orders signed. The judge reviews the papers you have submitted—sometimes from the bench, sometimes in chambers; it depends on the judge. If the judge takes the bench while you are in the courtroom, stand when the judge enters unless the bailiff says, "Remain seated." If your case is called, approach the bench, take your papers with you, and stand behind the "Petitioner" sign. Wait to see if the judge has any questions. If there are questions, you may be asked to answer them on the record under oath, or you may be asked to file an additional declaration. This is why you need two blank declaration forms with you. If asked to do so, you can make an additional declaration right there on the spot.

After the judge has considered your application, he or she will issue an order that day or the next day. It is required by law that the court rule on your application the same or the next day. The judge could possibly decide to issue temporary orders for a short time only and require further notice, but more likely he or she will grant the orders requested until the date set for a full hearing. Either way, make sure you understand the orders issued.

Get a date for the full hearing. The judge might set the date for the full hearing, or they might send you back to the clerk's office to get a hearing date. It will be in about 21 to 28 days. Make sure you can appear on the date they want to set. If you are not available on that day, say so.

Get five certified copies of the Order. Ask the clerk in the courtroom to give you five certified, stamped and endorsed copies of the Order To Show Cause and Temporary Restraining Order. You are entitled by law (Family Code section 6387) to up to five free certified copies and you definitely want them all. You take some of them to law enforcement agencies as explained below.

Keep a certified copy of your Order with you at all times. If you ever call the police out, it will help if you can show your Order to the responding officers.

Get two conformed copies of the entire set. Apart from the certified copies of the Order, you will also need two conformed copies of the entire set for your records and to use to make further copies. This is why you brought two copies of the whole set with you in addition to the originals. Make sure you have all the copies conformed by the clerk—file stamped, showing the date filed, and any other entries made by judges or clerks—before you leave the courtroom.

Sometimes a clerk will take your neatly packaged set of forms, tear it apart and conform the copies in his or her own mysterious way. Then you get everything back in a jumble. This is why you already have an orderly list of your forms with you so you can easily staple your sets back together again the way *you* want them.

Payroll subpoena. If you completed the payroll subpoena papers (Appendix C), go to the *filing window clerk* and file them now to have the subpoena issued. Have a copy of it served on Respondent's employer and include a copy with the papers that will be served on Respondent. If Respondent was already served with a copy of the initial papers, get your support person to mail a copy of the payroll subpoena to him and complete the Certificate of Compliance.

Make sure you do not leave the courthouse until you have five certified copies of the Order and two complete sets of conformed copies of all forms.

Take copies of the Orders to police

Immediately after leaving the court, deliver certified copies of the Order to each law enforcement agency that has jurisdiction near where you live, work and shop. If you live or work near a border between two police agencies, say the police and the sheriff, take one to each agency. If the police insist on proof that Respondent was served, return later with a conformed copy of the Proof of Service.

In L.A. County, the police agencies will also want a completed DVRO-Law Enforcement form containing your name and details that help identify Respondent—physical description, Social Security number, auto license and driver's license numbers. These forms are available at the clerk's office and at police stations. You can fill one out ahead of time or at the police station when you deliver your Order.

Prepare for the hearing

Next, you have to arrange to have papers served on Respondent as described in Chapter 18. It is now time to start preparing for your hearing. This takes a lot of careful thought and planning, so go to Chapter 19 as soon as possible and get started.

Chapter 18

Serving papers on Respondent

In all cases, Respondent must be personally handed the set of papers described below by someone over 18 other than yourself. If Respondent might show up at the ex parte hearing, you can make service then and there, so take a friend along and a complete set of papers to hand Respondent.

Here's how it works.

Who can serve the Respondent

Papers can be served by anyone over 18 who is not a party. That means you can't do it because you are a party (the Petitioner), but a friend or relative can, or the Marshal's office will do it for a small fee, or a professional process server will do it for somewhat more. The best thing is to get a friend or relative to do it if they will take the job seriously, work at it, do it quickly, and if it isn't dangerous for them to contact the Respondent.

The Marshal's office is not known for speed or efficiency in getting papers served, so it might be better if you can get a friend or professional to do it. The low fee is the attraction here. In Los Angeles County, the Marshal's fee is $24, and if you are *very* poor, you can file an application to have this fee waived. Ask the clerk at the filing windows for fee waiver forms; complete them, file them with your first set of papers and ask the court for a fee waiver order on the first day in court.

To find a professional process server, call any reliable attorney's office and ask the legal secretary who they use. Or just look in the phone book in the yellow pages. Give them a call; ask how much they charge and how quickly they can do it.

What papers are served

Never serve originals. All the papers served are *copies* of documents you filed that have been conformed by the clerk; that is, file stamped, showing the date filed, the hearing date written in, the judges name stamped in, and any other entries made by judges or clerks. Check the stamped date as clerks have been known to occasionally get this wrong. The set of papers that are served on Respondent should include:

✦ Declaration Re Ex Parte Notice.

✦ Application and Declarations (with the Declaration Under UCCJA if you had to use it).

✦ Order To Show Cause and Temporary Restraining Order with any attached pages, signed by the judge.

✦ Restraining Order After Hearing, with any attached pages.

✦ A blank Responsive Declaration.

✦ *If you are asking for child support:* include your completed set and a blank set of the Income and Expense Declaration forms.

✦ Local forms, if used in your county. For example, in Los Angeles County, you use the Certificate of Assignment in every case.

✦ *If you filed any supplemental declarations (Chapter 19):* include declarations.

✦ *If you subpoena payroll records (Appendix C):* include subpoena set.

If you use the Marshal or a professional process server, also include a photo of Respondent, a detailed description (age, race, height, weight, color of hair and eyes, glasses? scars?), home and work addresses, work hours, places where he hangs out regularly, and any other ideas you have about where and when he can be found.

When papers must be served

Papers *must* be served on Respondent on or before a certain day. The date of the hearing is written on the face of the Order to Show Cause, and item (11), on the back, shows how many days before the hearing Respondent must be served. That's your deadline, but don't leave it until the last minute, because it just means more work for you and the server if you don't get it done on time.

If you have a friend serve the papers, it is ideal if, on the day of your ex parte hearing, that person can take papers to be served directly from the courthouse to Respondent's home or place of work and serve him. If Respondent can't be found, try again. If Respondent still can't be found, you have a choice: keep trying or get the Marshal's office or a private process server to serve him. Some people try all three at the same time.

If Respondent can't be served on time

If Respondent can't be served before the deadline, go to the hearing and take along the Reissuance of Order to Show Cause form (Chapter 16F). Explain to the judge everything that was done to try to serve him. The judge will set another hearing date and extend your temporary orders. Ask for an additional 60 days and try to serve him again. If you still can't serve him, consider hiring a paralegal or a professional process server to arrange service by publication.

How to serve papers

If you decide to have a friend or relative do the service, give them the papers listed above and tell them that all they have to do is to personally hand the papers to Respondent. Once Respondent knows that court papers are being presented, it is his duty to accept them. If he doesn't, that's his problem. If he resists being served, the server should do this: once Respondent has been positively identified by sight or voice, the server should say, "I have court papers for you." If Respondent won't open the door, or refuses to take the papers, or if he turns and runs, or in any other way tries to avoid service, the server can just drop the papers in the nearest convenient spot where they can be found, then leave, and service has been effectively completed. Also mail a set to be on the safe side and note this in the Proof of Service.

Make sure the Proof of Service is filled out properly (Chapter 15E), dated and signed by the server.

File the Proof of Service

Make two copies of the Proof of Service and file these papers with the court clerk. Get a conformed copy of the Proof of Service. If Respondent does not appear at the noticed hearing, it is essential that you have either a conformed copy or, if it hasn't been filed yet, the original. The court will proceed only if it sees that Respondent had proper notice of the hearing.

If you do not have the Proof of Service on file, or if the court has misplaced it and you do not have a conformed copy, you have to set a new date, have your temporary orders extended, and serve him again. You can see how important it is to file the original and bring a conformed copy to the hearing.

Now go on to Chapter 19 to see what you need to be doing until the hearing date.

Chapter 19

Preparing for your hearing

Every day, thousands of people go to court and present their own cases, so you can certainly do it, too. A good attorney will prepare a case before trial, and this is what you are going to do—get yourself organized and prepared. In Chapter 7, you learned how to build your case. This chapter is where you learn how to prepare and present the evidence you have gathered.

Start your preparation immediately after the ex parte hearing, if not sooner, because there isn't much time. After working through this chapter, you may find that you need to file additional papers, and you must do so in time to get them served on Respondent before the deadline for service has passed (Chapter 18).

How facts are raised

A case is made up of facts. The facts you intend to prove are first stated in your Application and additional declarations, if any, made by yourself or other witnesses. The Application and additional declarations are filed with the court and served on Respondent to give him notice of what your case is about. If you go to court and start trying to state facts that were not previously raised, it makes a bad impression and weakens your case. This is why you need to think carefully, in advance, of all the facts you intend to prove. If anything has been left out, you can raise additional facts (see below), but you don't have much time to do it.

Review the facts you have raised

Of course, you can only present whatever facts you have, but you must make sure you have raised all available facts that will help your case.

List the orders you want. Review your proposed Order After Hearing and make a list of each order you are asking for.

List the facts you raised. Your job in court is to raise facts and present evidence that justifies each and every term of the orders you requested. Review your statements in the Application and any attached Declarations. Enter each fact you raised on your list alongside the related order you are seeking. Your list might look something like this, except that more detail would be better:

Order requested	Facts that justify the order
Restraining orders	Several violent incidents; threats; damage
100-yard stay-away	Repeated harassment, stalking me on street
Kick-out order	Kids enrolled in good local schools; he has parents' home near his work; my cancelled checks for rent payments
Child custody	Age of kids; he rarely cares for kids
Supervised visitation	Threats to take them and run; past abuse
Child support	Income and Expense Decs, pay stubs, tax returns
Use of the automobile	He has a truck; I need to drive kids around
Guns turned over to the police	He owns two pistols; threats when drunk
Medical insurance for children	Available through his union; already on it
Respondent to pay certain bills	Receipts for doctors and repairs for damage

Get in the judge's shoes and look at your case from her perspective. Ask yourself if the facts stated in your court forms seem strong enough to support the order requested. If you were the judge, would *you* grant the requested order based on the information you have presented?

The Judge will consider how big an intrusion each order is on Respondent. For example:

✦ Restraining and stay-away orders: not much abuse need be proved to get a restraining order. It doesn't impose much on Respondent to order him to leave you in peace.

✦ Guns. Owning a gun is not a right, so you should be able to get the abuser ordered to surrender his gun simply by showing he actually owns one and has threatened to use it on you.

✦ A kick-out order is a major imposition, so the facts listed above may not get a kick-out order. You need to show that there has been violence and that you are likely to be harmed if he stays, that you have no other place to go, and that you have a right to be there. It helps to also show that he has a place to go. (See Chapter 11-6.) If you can truthfully assert such facts, you need to add them to your case.

✦ A request for supervised visitation is a huge intrusion on the father's relationship with his children, so judges are reluctant to grant it if a narrower order will do. Your facts have to show that the children are in danger of being neglected, abused, or kidnapped if the visits are not monitored. If the Application doesn't make this clear, ask yourself if there are any additional facts that you can add that will help.

Courts that don't take testimony

If your case is being heard in a court that does not take "live" testimony (see Chapter 14), your declarations and documents carry the whole burden of making your case. By now you should have found out if this procedure will be followed in your court. If so, you should be extra careful to get all important facts presented in the form of declarations. If necessary, you can file additional declarations and serve them on Respondent if you can get it done before the time for serving Respondent has passed (see below).

Consider the response

In preparing your case, it is important to know if Respondent is going to put on a case, too. You will want to know what facts he is claiming in his statements and declarations so you can prepare your case accordingly. His response may cause you to file additional declarations (see below) to strengthen your case in areas where his statements of facts conflict with yours.

If Respondent is going to appear, he is supposed to serve you with a copy of his Responsive Declaration; however, it is not unusual for a Respondent to neglect to do this. In such a case, you are entitled to a continuance to further prepare, but this means another return to court and more lost time. If you don't want to come back again, get a copy of the Response and prepare your case in light of whatever you learn from it.

Before the hearing, go to the clerk's office and look at your case file to see if Respondent has filed a Responsive Declaration. Check back from time to time. Ask the clerk if you can do this by phone in the future.

How to raise additional facts

Applications are often completed in haste and under pressure from some emergency situation. Sometimes important facts are left out that would help the judge understand better why you need the requested orders. Sometimes facts claimed in the Response can inspire you to file additional declarations. If you can now think of any additional facts that would make your case stronger, you have a chance to add them to the record by filing additional declarations from yourself or any witnesses you may have. If you do, be sure to add any new facts raised to your list of facts.

To add additional facts, use the Declaration form (Chapter 16E) for statements of yourself or any witnesses you may have. File each one with the clerk and serve it on Respondent. The rule is that these must be filed and served five court days in advance of the hearing. If it isn't possible for you to do this on time, file and serve them as soon as possible before the hearing and hope the judge admits them anyway. If they are rejected, you can ask permission to present testimony, request a continuance, or go with what is in the court's file.

You can see that you don't have much time to get all this done, so you will want to give careful thought to your case as early as possible in the process.

How to prove facts at the hearing

Study your list of facts you want to prove and decide how you will prove each one. There are two basic ways to prove a fact: with documents, and through the testimony of yourself and any witnesses you have. You can use either one or both at the same time. More than one witness can testify to the same fact.

We are going to describe the correct way to make your case in court. In real life, people sometimes fall short of the ideal. Declarations are incomplete, witnesses don't show, documents can't be found. Whatever happens, give it your best and let the judge decide what to do with what you present.

Witnesses

Ideally, any witnesses will already have made statements on a Declaration form as described above. Unless the court is one of those that does not take live testimony at a DVRO hearing (see Chapter 14), you should also arrange for each witness to be at the hearing, if possible. The judge may want to ask questions and Respondent has a right to cross-examine. If a witness doesn't show, the judge may or may not consider the statements in that witness's declaration. At the very least, the weight given it will be somewhat lower.

Using child witnesses. Generally, the court does not want to hear from your children unless there is no other way to prove child abuse or violence against you in their presence. Even then, the child has to be old enough to know the difference between telling the truth and telling a lie. Another exception might be for older children who want to express their own preferences for custody and visitation.

Children are damaged by observing abuse and can be further damaged by being made to testify against a parent or relive their trauma in a courtroom. Besides, using them this way can backfire; having a child testify against a parent is disturbing, and if there is even a hint that the child is being used or that the child has been coached, the judge might well rule against the parent who is perceived as manipulating and misusing the child.

An alternative is to have the children interviewed by a doctor or psychologist who can make a declaration as to the condition of the children, including their state of mind and what they said. Such an interview should only be done by a qualified child therapist.

The judge may want to speak to the children, but can do so only if the parties agree. You should decide in advance whether this is a good idea and be prepared to deal with this issue if the judge asks. If the judge decides to interview the children, be prepared for them to have their own thoughts which they might not have shared with you. If so, do not punish or scorn the child for having his or her own opinions; this will only alienate the child.

When you testify, don't argue

You need to understand the difference between testimony and argument. You get to do both, but not at the same time. When you are presenting your case, you are strictly dealing in facts. Testimony means that a witness can state facts directly observed first hand—what he or she personally saw and heard—without conclusions or interpretation. Later, after all evidence is presented by both sides, the judge will listen to your argument. Argument is when you explain how you interpret the facts presented and give the conclusions you want the judge to draw.

For example:

> **The facts:** Your Honor, Respondent is living in a camper on the back of his truck which he parks each night at various places on the streets. It is only about ten feet long and six feet wide. There is no bathroom in it.

> **The argument:** Your Honor, Respondent shouldn't have overnight visits because he has no proper place for the children to sleep. He lives in a small camper parked on public streets with no bathroom in it. That is not a suitable place to care for children.

When you actually testify, relax. Most judges will help you get your story out.

Documents

If you have documents to present, bring the original and two copies of each: one copy for Respondent and one for your own records. A document is introduced during the testimony of a witness who can identify it and tell the judge what it is.

When you present a document, first offer the original to the judge and have the bailiff or clerk pass a copy to Respondent. Tell the judge what the document is, and say, "I'd like to have this marked for identification," and the clerk will give it an exhibit number. The witness then tells the judge what the document is about, what it shows, and where it came from. If the judge has further questions about a document, he'll ask. Before you move on to another point, say, "Your Honor, I'd like to have this document admitted into evidence."

For example, you would introduce your bills and receipts to prove expenses, and canceled rent checks with your signature to prove you have a right to reside in a house if you are seeking a kick-out order. Another witness would identify photos she took of you after a beating and say they accurately show the way you looked.

Medical bills and injuries. You can generally prove injuries simply by testifying about them. Photos will help if you have any. If you have copies of medical reports, offer them to the court and ask that they be introduced. If the doctor is not present in court (not easy to arrange) the medical reports are open to challenge, but you can let the judge deal with that. If you want Respondent to pay your medical bills, bring copies of the bills and introduce them.

Payroll subpoenas. If you subpoenaed Respondent's payroll records, call the employer to make sure these will get to the court in time for the hearing. Ask that they be sent by priority mail. They have to be delivered by independent means; you can't pick up and deliver them yourself. On the deadline, call the court and make sure they have arrived.

Employers are under subpoena to appear if they do not produce the records after having been given a reasonable time, about 20 days. If they have had the subpoena more than 20 days, remind them of this and suggest they deliver the records to the court clerk by messenger if they don't want to show up in court to explain why the documents are not there. If they have had less than 20 days to respond, you would be unwise to push them.

If subpoenaed records do not arrive in time for the hearing, and if you can't show Respondent's income any other way, show the court the subpoena and ask to have the hearing and the temporary orders continued for two weeks.

Make a trial outline and practice your presentation

You have already made a list of all the facts you are going to raise and prove. Now make a list of your witnesses, starting with yourself, in the order you want them to appear. For each witness, add a list of each fact that witness will testify to and each document that witness will introduce, in logical order. Make sure every important fact is on this list and check each one off as it goes by in your presentation. This is your trial outline and it is very important. It will keep you from getting flustered or forgetting anything in court.

Documents are normally introduced during the testimony of the person who can identify them and say what they represent. You can introduce your bills, receipts, and other documents that prove expenses you incurred because of the abuser. You could identify a photo and say that it accurately reflects the way you looked at the time, or the photo could be introduced by the person who took it.

You want to tell your story in a coherent order that the judge can follow. Start with who you are and describe your relationship with Respondent. Tell about the events that caused you to file for a DVRO, then go back to the beginning and work your way to the present. Tell about repeated acts, threats, and harm caused. Use documents and witnesses to fill in details that support your story. Make sure that every fact you need to prove is listed so you can check each one off as you proceed through the hearing.

Review your case with your legal clinic counselor or someone in your support group or a friend. Ask them to read this chapter and go over your case with you. Make sure your list of facts raised is complete.

Practice. Once you have organized the facts you want to prove, how you will prove them, and the order of presentation at trial, practice what you are going to say to the judge and how you are going to tell your story. Do it in front of a mirror or into a tape recorder. Better yet, practice with a friend or someone from your support group. Read Chapter 20 so you understand what will happen at the hearing.

Go observe a hearing

If you can take the time, you will gain a lot from going to the same courtroom where your hearing will be heard to observe other people going through the same process. Some will have attorneys; many will be doing it alone. Talk to the clerks and bailiffs. Find out ahead of time how it looks and feels. Get some ideas about how you will do things.

If you can't observe a hearing before your own, call a local domestic violence clinic or hotline in your area and ask what this particular judge expects. Someone in your support group or at the shelter should be able to give you some information.

Chapter 20

What to do at the hearing and afterward

Your first trip to the courtroom, when the judge signed your Order to Show Cause, was called the ex parte hearing. This one is called the *noticed* hearing, so called because Respondent had full notice and more opportunity to show up and tell his side. The judge will take a longer look at the facts, especially if Respondent presents a case. This chapter is about what happens at a noticed hearing.

Check in

Be sure you show up on time, maybe even a little early, with your witnesses and support person. Wear comfortable, conservative clothing. Have your files with you, having checked the day before to make sure everything you need is there and organized for easy access:

✦ your trial outline and checklist (Chapter 19)

✦ conformed copies of all forms you have already filed with the court

✦ all photos and documents you plan to present (original and two copies of each)

✦ blank declaration forms and black ballpoint pen. If Respondent was not served on time, also bring an Application for Reissuance (Chapter 16F)

As soon as you arrive, check in with the clerk or bailiff who will probably ask to see your Proof of Service if it is not already in the court file. If you have one, file it at this time and make sure you get your copies conformed. If Respondent was not served, present your Application for Reissuance (Chapter 16F) at this time.

If you have additional declarations to file, do so and make sure you have copies to give to Respondent. If you subpoenaed Respondent's payroll records, ask the clerk to check the evidence envelopes to see if your payroll records are in. If not, you have to decide whether to proceed or ask for a continuance. Ask the judge for advice if you're not sure what to do.

Now you just sit and wait until your case is called. Watch the way the court handles the cases that go before yours. You might learn something useful.

When your case is called

When you hear your case called, you and your support person go up to the counsel table, greet the judge, and tell him you are ready to proceed: "Good morning, your Honor. I am the Petitioner, appearing *in pro per* and I am ready to proceed." You will probably be asked to state and spell your name for the record. You may be referred to as the Protected Party, or the Petitioner. If the judge asks you for a time estimate, tell her how many people will testify on your side. You might be asked to proceed at once or, more likely, you might be asked to wait for second call. Whatever, just say, "Thank you, your Honor," and do as directed.

If Respondent has not appeared

If Respondent is not in court when the case is called, the judge or clerk will check the file for the Proof of Service. The case may be passed to a second call.

Respondent not served. If you do not have a Proof of Service and Respondent does not appear, the court will set a new hearing date and continue your temporary orders. You will have to complete and file an Application for Reissuance (Chapter 16F). Get the copies conformed and include a copy of it with the other papers being served on Respondent.

Respondent served. If, for whatever reason, the Proof isn't in the file, the court will ask you for it. Hand over either the original and two copies or your file-stamped copy showing that the original was filed. Make sure you get your copy back or a conformed copy of the original. This is very important.

Once the court confirms that Respondent was served and that he has not appeared, the judge might ask you to proceed at once, but it is also common to be asked to wait, until second call of the cases. Whenever your case is called, be prepared to proceed.

If Respondent shows up

In order to be heard, Respondent must have filed a written Response and served you with a copy of it so you can see what his story is. If he tries to present a Response for the first time at the hearing, ask the judge for a few minutes to study it. Now you have to decide whether you want to go ahead anyway or ask for a continuance to give you time to prepare for Respondent's case.

If Respondent has filed his Response and is in court, all this means is that the judge is going to consider both sides before making a decision and issuing orders.

If Respondent brings an attorney, you can ask the court for a continuance to seek counsel yourself. However, if you are well-prepared, there is no need to panic. Some people *in pro per* do very well even when there is an attorney on the other side. Whether to go ahead or not is a personal decision, depending on your degree of confidence.

Before making a final decision, you can assess the situation further by asking the judge to set your case to the back of the calendar so you can have a chance to talk with Respondent's attorney. One advantage of Respondent having an attorney is that you can negotiate without having to speak directly with your abuser. You can get a sense of what the attorney is like, his or her attitude, and what they hope to accomplish in court. Then you can decide whether to proceed or ask for a continuance so you can get your own attorney. This is what you do:

> With your support person present—but without Respondent—go somewhere where you can talk. Ask the attorney if there are any parts of your proposed Order After Hearing that Respondent can agree to. For those orders he objects to, ask for details—what, exactly, his position is. When the attorney replies, listen carefully; write it all down.
>
> If there are some parts of the Order you can agree to—with or without

changes—and some you can't, and if Respondent's attorney is willing, you can tell the judge about the orders you agree to and limit the hearing to just those orders you were unable to agree on. For example, let's say the Respondent agrees to move out in two weeks instead of immediately and you decide you can accept this change. He also agrees to let you have custody of the children and pay guideline support, but he refuses to pay certain bills. The hearing can proceed now solely on the issue of the bills.

However, Respondent's attorney might agree to some things only on the condition that you give in on others. Don't give in on issues that are important to you. If it turns out that nothing is agreed to, you simply proceed with the whole case, just as you always intended. Don't get pressured into going against your own best interest.

The next time your case is called, go up and either ask for a continuance so you can get an attorney or tell the judge you are ready to proceed.

If child custody is an issue. If Respondent shows up and child custody is an issue, you will probably be asked if you have been through conciliation court (mediation) on the issue. If not, you might be sent immediately to a mediation session just on the child custody issue. The parties will be ordered to return to court afterward; if not, remind the judge to make this important order because you want to be sure Respondent returns. When you go to mediation, you do not have to meet together with Respondent if you do not want to. If mediation succeeds, you will return to court with an agreement on custody and visitation, ready to present your case on other issues. If mediation fails, you will return to court ready to proceed on all issues. Chances are you will be able finish your hearing on the same day, but if not, the judge will order the parties to return on another date to finish the hearing and order the continuation of the temporary orders until then. Respondent should be present in court to hear this.

Presenting your case

Present your case as described in Chapter 19. Whether or not Respondent is present, you still have to make your case. Testimony is heard from yourself and any other witnesses and documents are introduced into evidence. Just facts.

During your presentation, Respondent is allowed to cross-examine (ask questions of) you and your witnesses after testimony. If Respondent is present, you can call him to the stand as part of your case or you can wait to see what he does when it is his turn and then cross-examine.

You can choose to submit your case entirely on the declarations. Refer to the Orders After Hearing, already on file, and tell the judge that you want the court to grant the proposed order based on your declarations. Say, "Your Honor, I am asking for orders that are supported by the facts stated in my declarations on file. I would like to submit this matter on the declarations."

Respondent puts on his case. If Respondent is present and puts on a case, his testimony will probably contradict evidence in your case—why else would he show up? This is why you want multiple witnesses, photos and documents to help prove important facts. You can cross-examine Respondent and his witnesses if you think you can get them to say something that helps you, or if you want to try to develop enough details to make it more clear they are not telling a straight story. When done, Respondent rests his case.

Rebuttal. You can, if you wish, put on *new* evidence that directly contradicts anything in Respondent's case. Then you rest your case.

You argue your case. Interpret the facts, draw conclusions about what they mean, explain why your evidence is more believable than Respondent's. Explain why it is necessary to have the orders you want.

Respondent argues.

Rebuttal. You can respond briefly against specific points in Respondent's argument.

The judge rules and issues her order. The order will be signed. If you do not understand the order, ask the judge for further explanation. Be gracious and do not argue with the court. If you need an order that the court overlooked, ask for it. If you don't like the order the court made, don't show this openly. You might see this judge again some day for enforcement or for further family action. Be businesslike.

Variations

Some judges are relatively informal and will also relax the rules of evidence for people without attorneys; others are more formal and strict. Some judges will take an active role and generally guide things along in their own way; others will sit back and wait for you to put on a case. To be prepared means that you know your case very well, but you are also prepared to follow the judge's lead. If you were able to come in previously to observe cases in this courtroom, you will already have a good idea how this judge operates.

Courts that don't take testimony

We've mentioned it before: some judges don't hear testimony from witnesses in a DVRO case, but decide solely on the basis of written declarations and oral argument. If that is the case in your court, your case proceeds like this:

✦ hand the clerk to give to the judge whatever documents or photographs you may have (with copies for yourself and Respondent). As you hand each one over, explain to the judge what facts are proved with that item;

✦ if you subpoenaed payroll records, ask the court to examine them;

✦ offer additional declarations. They were supposed to have been filed and served on Respondent some days before the hearing, so some judges will refuse to admit them, but it does no harm to make the offer;

✦ move on to the argument phase. Refer to your proposed orders in the Restraining Order After Hearing. For each order, explain why you are asking for it and why it is reasonable or necessary for you to have it. That is your closing argument.

After the hearing

✦ Before you leave the courthouse, get five certified copies of the Order After Hearing and the Wage Assignment Order, too, if one was issued.

✦ Go immediately to the same police agencies as before (Chapter 17) and deliver copies of the Order. If Respondent was present in court, this will show on the face of the Order. Point this out to them. In L.A. County, you will once again have to file the DVRO–Legal Information form.

✦ If the children are protected in the Order, or if you are concerned that Respondent not have access them to them except as specified, take a copy of the Order to the children's school. Give complete instructions as to who can and cannot pick up the children.

✦ Consider giving a copy of the Order to the security people at work. If your residence has security, give them a copy, too. Put those on notice who can be of help to you in an emergency. Ask friendly neighbors to be alert and call the police if they hear sounds of violence from your place.

✦ Serve a conformed copy of the Wage Assignment Order on Respondent's employer by mail if one was issued. Complete a Proof of Service by mail, file it and keep a copy in your file.

✦ Serve Respondent. If Respondent was present in court when the order was issued, this will show on the face of the Order; he already knows about the Order so he does not have to be personally served. If Respondent did not appear, he *must* be personally served with a copy of the order in the same manner you used to serve him with the Order to Show Cause (Chapter 18). Make sure a Proof of Service form (Chapter 15E) is completed. File it and get conformed copies for the police. Take a copy of the Proof to the police with jurisdiction over your residence. This allows them to enter all the details of your order into the Department of Justice database which is used by all police agencies.

Practical steps

Prepare and file any further family law actions which you must file to complete this matter. If you have a child support and custody order, ask the court to consolidate the domestic violence action with the family law action.

Keep a conformed copy of the Order with you at all times. If you ever need to call the police to enforce your Order or protect yourself, it will help things along if you can show them the Order.

If Respondent violates the order, you can call the police and have him arrested and charged. It is a criminal matter and he can go to jail. Be sure to follow through. The police report that their greatest problem in domestic cases is that the victim does not cooperate in the prosecution of the case. Prove to them that this is not going to happen in your case. Cooperate with the City or District Attorney's office in any criminal action filed against Respondent.

Stay away from places you know Respondent frequents. Granted, you have the "right" to go anywhere you want, but it is better to be safe; this is just common sense. Your order does not make you bulletproof, and it won't keep you from getting hurt if you are attacked..

Shift your focus. Without reducing your vigilance against trouble, shift your focus away from Respondent as much as possible and get on with your own life. Make your growth and progress and that of your children your focus from now on.

> *"It has been three years. I have a job as a bookkeeper. It took me two years of community college courses to learn the skills. I am so proud. I will never get into an abusive relationship again. I know this. I have been in counseling for three years. I can see how what happened to me started, how it progressed, and I know now that it will never happen again. I will never let it happen again."*
>
> ——Martha

Recommended reading

These are fine books, but this is not an exhaustive list of literature on domestic violence. Go to any library or bookstore and see what's available.

Domestic abuse

The Battered Woman by Lenore E. Walker. Harper Perennial 1979.

The Battered Woman Syndrome by Lenore E. Walker. Springer Publishing 1984.

The Family Secret: Domestic Violence in America by William Stacey and Anson Shupe. Beacon Press 1983.

Family Violence by Richard J. Gelles. Sage Publications 1979.

International Perspectives on Family Violence. Edited by Richard J. Gelles and Clair Pedrick Cornell. Lexington Books 1983.

Violence in the Family, an Annotated Bibliography by Elizabeth Kemmer. Garland Publishing 1984.

It Could Happen to Anyone: Why Battered Women Stay by Ola W. Barnett and Alyce D. La Violette. Sage Publications 1993.

Battered Wives (revised and updated) by Del Martin. Volcano Press 1976, 1981.

The Battered Woman's Survival Guide: Breaking the Cycle, a Resource Manual for Victims, Relatives, Friends and Professionals by Jan Berliner Statman. Taylor Publishing 1990, 1995. This book contains a list of shelters and resources located in each state. It lists about 100 shelters for California.

Getting Free: You Can End Abuse and Take Back Your Life by Ginny NiCarthy. Seal Press 1986 (second edition).

Talking It Out: A Guide to Groups for Abused Women by Ginny NiCarthy, Karen Merriam and Sandra Coffman. New Leaf Series 1984.

Books in Spanish

Mejor sola que mal acompañada para la mujer golpeada by Myrna M. Zambrano. New Leaf 1985.

La mujer maltratada: Un estudio sobre las mujeres victimas de la violencia domestica by Gracilla B. Ferreira. Impreso en la Argentina, primera edición 1989, tercera edición 1994.

Regaining your personal power and reshaping your life

How to Get Control of Your Time and Your Life by Alan Lakein. Signet 1974. This is a classic.

The Survival Guide for Women: Single, Married, Divorced by Renee and Don Martin. Regnery Gateway.
By the same authors: *Protecting Your Future.*

The Seven Habits of Highly Effective People by Steven R. Covey. Simon & Schuster Fireside Editions 1990.

Your Erroneous Zones by Dr. Wayne W. Dyer. Avon 1976.
By the same author: *The Sky's the Limit* and *Pulling Your Own Strings.*

Parenting

How to Talk So Kids Will Listen and Listen So Kids Will Talk by Adele Faber and Elaine Mazlish. Rawson Associates, Simon & Schuster.

By the same authors: *How to Talk So Kids Can Learn, Liberated Parents/Liberated Children, Siblings Without Rivalry* and *Between Brothers and Sisters: A Celebration of Life's Most Enduring Relationship.*

Books and articles on relationships

Mandatory Custody Mediation and Joint Custody Orders in California: The Danger for Victims of Domestic Violence by Charlotte Germane, Margaret Johnson, and Nancy Lemon. Berkeley Women's Law Journal, Vol. 1/1, Fall 1985, p. 175. This article presented pivotal thinking which has since been adopted by the legislature in the protections for domestic violence victims in custody and visitation statutes.

Divorce Is Not the Answer: A Change of Heart Will Save Your Marriage by George S. Pransky, Ph.D. Human Services Institute, McGraw-Hill 1990. Do not let the title throw you. If you are routinely being hit and battered, this book is not recommended to you as a way of healing your relationship. This book explains why traditional relationship therapy has not worked, and offers a new approach which is more effective.

Conscious Loving: The Journey to Co-Commitment by Gay Hendricks, Ph.D. and Kathlyn Hendricks, Ph.D. Bantam Books 1992.

Appendix A

How to be a support person

If you have a friend who is struggling with an abusive relationship and you want to help, read this section—and more if you can. Do not be afraid to help. You may save a life.

Listen, without giving advice, judging or blaming

Be prepared to do a lot of listening. Do not judge her, or tell her what to do. Do not blame her. Do not expect your friend to do things the way you want her to do them. She has to find her own way. It may take her some time to leave the relationship and she may go back several times. This is normal. Do not give up on her if she goes back to him several times. Try to understand how hard it is to leave someone you once loved, your home and possessions; everything you have known, your security and income.

Keep your balance

Do not get too involved with her view of herself or her batterer. Listen to her, but form your own opinions and keep them to yourself. Keep your own balance. You may not find him to be very scary at all. This would be a normal reaction. If you do find him be a scary person, take practical precautions. Do not needlessly expose yourself to danger.

Do what you can

She may need someone to store papers, possessions, keys. She may need someone to take photographs of her bruises, take her to the doctor, the police, to mediation or to court.

Be her support person at court hearings

She will need someone who can attend hearings and mediation with her. This means driving to the courthouse with her and sitting in the courtroom, the hall, the cafeteria. It means staying with her like a shadow. You are an emotional bodyguard and a passive physical bodyguard. The support person, however, does not give advice or attempt to participate in the meetings or hearings. The support person is present and supportive, but not a participant.

Service of process

She may need a friend who can serve papers on her batterer (the Respondent) and who can fill out and sign the Proof of Service. These procedures are described in detail under Proof of Service in the instructions above.

Safe haven

She may need a place to stay. If you become the safe haven, do not disclose that she is with you or permit her to answer the phone, ever. If possible, her car should not be parked on the street. Look at the section on shelters and see what a safe place is.

Neutral transport

She may need someone who can pick up the children from school or attend to visits with the father. For the school, you need written permission from the mother delivered to the school along with a certified copy of any court order.

Planning

She may need someone to help her plan. If so, urge her to use someone trained in domestic violence counseling. This is a very specific problem and it takes time to understand how to work with it. You can help if you stand by and offer practical assistance now and then while your friend works out her plan.

Counseling

Encourage her to get into counseling and help her find a qualified counselor. Read the sections in this book on counseling.

Further support

If you would like to be of further support, consider attending a support group meeting or 12-step meeting with her. Read all of this book and look at the bibliography for further reading. Remember to keep your balance.

Appendix B

Mediation and parenting plans

Conciliation and mediation

If you have children with the abuser and custody arrangements are not agreed upon, mediation may be required before you get orders for child custody. Judges think custody is too important to decide in a few minutes of court time, especially if the parties can work it out between them with the help of a court-appointed mediator.

The way this works is different from county to county, so you need to ask about it the first time you go to a courtroom to get your papers signed by the judge. Be sure to ask the clerk or judge if you are required to attend conciliation or mediation before the hearing.

Here are the possibilities:

✦ You will be instructed to make a mediation appointment as soon as possible and try to complete mediation before the hearing.

✦ You will show up at the hearing and if Respondent is there, you will be asked to go immediately to see a mediator.

✦ You will not be required to mediate before the hearing.

In some counties you will be sent to "Family Conciliation Court" where the services are free. Others may refer you to a panel of mediators where the fees are either free or on a reasonable scale. From now on, let's just call it "mediation." In either case, both parents see a licensed counselor—a mediator—who helps develop a parenting plan. Parenting plans are discussed below. Financial issues are not covered, nor any other issue apart from custody and parenting arrangements.

You need not meet with the abuser. In domestic violence cases, you can request that the mediator meet with the parties separately (Family Code 3181). Be sure to make this request in advance. Similarly, a judge can order either or both of the parties into counseling, but if this happens you can request separate sessions (Family Code 3192).

You can bring a support person. You are entitled to have a support person with you at any hearing, mediation or counseling session (Family Code 6303). This person may not participate or give legal advice. If this person interferes, he or she can be asked to leave. If you are concerned about your safety or are frightened by the abuser, bring a support person to all hearings with you. Ask that person to read the support section in this book. Do not appear alone in any public place, court or parking lot during the active period of this case.

Confidentiality. Under State law, mediation sessions are confidential. However, in some counties, if mediation fails, the mediator makes a custody recommendation to the judge.

Agreement becomes Order. The mediator has no power to make orders but, if you do reach an agreement and sign a parenting plan, your agreed plan will become the order of the court. This is why you should be well prepared for the mediation session.

Just say no. Do not sign an agreement that you feel is wrong for the children and the family. It is better to ask for a second conciliation or work it out in court than to sign off on a bad plan. At the very least, confer with counsel before you sign a plan that you aren't comfortable with. On the other hand, there are so many advantages to settling by agreement that you should not hesitate to be flexible and make *reasonable* compromises to get one.

Prepare for the appointment. Go to your mediation appointment with one or two alternate plans in mind. Work out what you want to do in advance and write it down. This will help you think more clearly when you are meeting with the mediator. List the reasons you want certain terms and conditions. Do not get stuck on one idea, but have several alternatives in mind. If the going gets tough, consider making a temporary plan, then agree to return for further mediation.

How to make a parenting plan

Legal rights. Your parenting plan should start out by defining the rights of the parents in the legal terms defined in Chapter 11(2). Write down who will have legal custody of the child and who will have physical custody. For example:

> "The parents shall have joint legal custody of Jeremy Jones with sole physical custody to Mother."

However, no matter what the legal terms are, when it comes to day-by-day child care, the thing that counts most is your parenting plan. A parenting plan includes a detailed schedule of when each parent has the privilege and the responsibility of caring for the child. You want to know which parent is responsible every moment of the child's days and nights.

Designated parent. Your parenting plan should cover time when the child is in school, child care, at lessons or extracurricular activities. Who will be called in case of illness or injury? The parent on duty should be defined in the plan.

Modifications. The most important thing about parenting plans is to remember that you can always depart from the schedule by mutual agreement at any time. But when you do not agree to a variation, you have to follow the plan. It has already been agreed to and ordered by a judge.

General guidelines. A very young child should have more frequent, shorter visits, so that bonding can be maintained or cultivated. This can be a problem where the distance between parents is large. Where the parents live near each other, a plan that includes substantial weekly time for each parent is workable. Where the parents live far apart, one parent tends to keep the child most of the school year, but extended periods of time with the other parent can be arranged for long holidays, summers, and school breaks.

Timeshare. Once you have a schedule, you can add up the percentage of the year that each parent has the care of the child. This is called "timeshare" and is part of the formula for figuring out the correct amount of child support. This number should be figured and stated in your parenting plan. The computer program CalSupport, available from Nolo Press, contains a KidCare™ feature that will help you work out your schedule and calculate timeshare at the same time. See the inside front cover for more information.

Parenting schedule and timeshare worksheet
Schedule for (name of child or children)

Define the schedule for the parent with the least care time (sometimes called the "noncustodial" parent). If different children will have different schedules, simply make as many different schedules as necessary.

1. Weekend care will take place:

a. ☐ every weekend ☐ on alternate weekends ___ weekends per year

b. The typical or average weekend care period will be ___ days and ___ hours and is defined as follows: (state when and where it begins and ends).

2. Midweek care will take place:

a. ☐ every week ☐ on alternate weeks ___ weeks per year

b. The typical or average midweek care period will be ___ days and ___ hours and is defined as follows: (state when and where it begins and ends).

3. Summer care will be ___ weeks each summer.

a. During the summer care period, the parent with primary care will have the child(ren) for visits for a total of ___ days and ___ hours.

b. ___ days and ___ hours counted in the summer schedule have already been counted in either of the weekly schedules.

Consider the effect of summer camps and summer classes.

4. Holiday care: Indicate how each holiday will be scheduled. Longer holidays can by split, part with one parent and part with the other, or alternated: even years with Mom, odd years with Dad. Shorter holidays can be alternated.

For figuring timeshare, enter the average time for care over two years. Be very careful not to count days already counted in the weekly or summer schedules. For example, if Dad takes the child every weekend for 2 days and every Thanksgiving for 4 days, enter 2 care days for Thanksgiving because 2 of the 4 Thanksgiving days were already counted as part of the weekend schedule.

Holiday:	Standard school holiday	Mom, Dad, split or alternate (describe how it will work)	Average days per year in addition to regular weekly/summer schedule
Spring break (Easter)	7	_____	_____
New Year's break	14	_____	_____
Labor Day weekend	3	_____	_____
Memorial Day weekend	3	_____	_____
Fourth of July weekend	3	_____	_____
Thanksgiving	4	_____	_____

Other holidays: Whatever the family celebrates, depending on job, religion or cultural background: Martin Luther King's Day, President's Day, Ramadan, etc.)

1._____   _____   _____

2._____   _____   _____

3._____   _____   _____

Mother's and Father's Days are usually spent with the parent whose day it is. Agree to switch weekends whenever necessary to accomodate these days.

Child's birthday. One solution is to simply follow the regular schedule and the parent with whom the child is scheduled has the birthday that year and the other parent simply celebrates on the next closest day he or she is with the child. Some families alternate birthdays, others include both parents in all birthday celebrations.

Parents' birthdays. Children are typically with a parent on his or her own birthday, but that time is not counted in the calculation of timeshare.

Extracurricular activities. Sports, school clubs and other outside activities should not be allowed to interfere with the non-custodial parent's time unless arranged by prior agreement.

Notice of address changes and moves. Parents should agree not to take the child out of state for more than *x* days, or not at all, without 30 days' written notice to the other parent. Similarly, if children are being cared for at Dad's residence, he should agree to give 45 days' written notice of where and when he intends to move. Mom should make the same agreement unless she is keeping her address confidential.

Other child care issues

Transportation. Who will transport the children? Generally the receiving parent picks up or pays for transportation.

Cost of travel for visitation. Who will pay for transportation if the parties live far enough apart that there is a need for public transport? Can the children travel alone or will they need a paid escort?

Telephone access. Will both parents have free telephone access to the children? As long as basic ground rules can be created, the visiting parent should have free telephone access to the children.

Clothes, toys. Each parent should buy and care for their own set of clothes and toys for the children. Special equipment can be shared, but some families duplicate everything; less to disagree about.

Long-term planning

These issues come under the heading of "legal custody" and are about long-term child-rearing issues such as education, religion, schooling, and health care. Some parenting plans include agreements on these matters.

Education. Where and how the children are to be educated. Public or private school, which school, what course of study.

Religious training. This is not usually covered in a parenting plan because the law is clear that each parent is entitled to share his or her religion with the children. Courts have held that exposure to differing religious views is not confusing to children, absent some very special circumstances.

Medical treatment. In an emergency, either parent should be able to act. Any other treatment should be discussed with the other parent first. Deductibles and expenses not covered by insurance are generally shared.

Miscellaneous advice

Parent communications. Do not communicate through the children. This puts a strain on them, and angers the other parent. If you have business to take care of and do not want to talk directly, write a note. If necessary, send it by certified mail; request return receipt if you want proof of your communication. Some families simply make phone calls. Use your judgment. The point is, leave the children out of it.

Positive reinforcement. Some plans include a statement, "Neither party shall make derogatory remarks about the other parent within the presence or hearing of the children. Disagreements will not be conducted in view or hearing of the children."

Appendix C

How to subpoena payroll records

If you request child support, you need documents that prove his income. If you have no other way to get records—pay stubs, tax returns, bank statements—and if he is employed and you can find out the name and address of his employer, then you can subpoena his payroll records. They will be sent to the court under seal to be opened on the day of the hearing. Most employers are familiar with these requests and will cooperate.

You need to start the subpoena process as far in advance of the hearing as possible, because the employer needs time to forward the records. If possible, get these papers processed by the clerk and served on Respondent along with your other DVRO papers. Give the employer 20 days advance notice if possible, but no less than 10 days at minimum. The more the better.

The forms

Here is a simple set of forms you can use to have a subpoena issued by the clerk the same day you go in to file your application for a DVRO—or any time later.

1. **Declaration Application for Subpoena Duces Tecum.** This is your request for the subpoena and your statements to justify it.

2. **Civil Subpoena.** The clerk signs this form to issue the subpoena.

3. **Notice to Respondent.** Tells Respondent his records are being subpoenaed.

4. **Proof of Service.** On the back of the Civil Subpoena; the server signs it after service is completed.

5. **Petitioner's Declaration Re Compliance.** This shows the employer that Respondent has been served with copies of subpoena papers and on what day.

6. **Employer's Declaration Re Compliance.** This is to be completed by the employer's payroll officer (AKA Custodian of Record). You serve them with a blank form to help the process along case they don't have one of their own.

Complete the papers and get the subpoena issued

Complete the first three forms as shown in the illustrations. Make two copies of each one and take them to the clerk. It's most efficient if you can do this when you file your other papers on your first trip to court, but they can be issued and served at any later time as well. Subpoena papers are not filed, but they are stamped and "issued" by the clerk. You keep the originals; the court will want to see them if the records do not appear at the time of the hearing.

Complete the headings on the remaining forms. Add the case number if you already have it. Don't give your address if it is kept confidential on the other documents in your case. Type in Respondent's name at the first blank on form 3, the Notice. Type in your name at the first blank on form 5, Petitioner's Declaration. Leave everything else blank, to be completed later.

Serve Respondent and the employer

Note: You keep all originals plus one complete copy. Only copies are served. If the subpoena is questioned, you must be able to show the court what papers were served and for this you need the original Proof of Service, signed.

Have someone serve Respondent with conformed copies (stamped by the clerk) of the first three forms. After Respondent is served, you date and sign Petitioner's Declaration re Compliance.

Have someone go with you to wherever Respondent's payroll department is and have the server hand the subpoena papers to the payroll officer (the Custodian of Records in court lingo). In a small enough company, this could be the boss himself. The employer's officer receives copies of:

✦ Civil Subpoena

✦ Declaration Application

- ✦   Notice to Respondent
- ✦   Petitioner's Declaration re Compliance
- ✦   A blank copy of Employer's Declaration

If Respondent works at the same location and is present, you can serve him with all papers and then go do the employer.

Have your support person complete the Proof of Service on the back of the Subpoena. Keep the original and take it with you on the day of the hearing.

Follow-up

Three days after serving employer, call the payroll officer and ask if the records were forwarded to the court. If not, explain that the hearing is coming soon and ask politely for their cooperation. Call back in a few days to see how things are going. As your hearing date nears, go to the clerk's office and ask to see your file to check if the records have been received. Ask the clerk if you can check on this by phone or if you have to come in each time.

At the hearing

If the records show up in time, at the hearing you will ask the judge to open the sealed envelope and admit the records into evidence.

If the records do not show up in time, you have to decide whether to proceed with what evidence and testimony you have or ask for a continuance to try to get compliance with the subpoena. Tell the judge what evidence you have and ask if she will be willing to hear the support issue without the payroll records.

Figure C-1: Declaration Application for Subpoena Duces Tecum

ATTORNEY OR PARTY WITHOUT ATTORNEY *(Name and Address)*:	TELEPHONE NO.:	FOR COURT USE ONLY
—Virginia E. 12345 South Street City, State, Zip	(000)000-00000	

ATTORNEY FOR *(Name)*: Virginia E., In Pro Per

NAME OF COURT: Los Angeles County Superior Court
STREET ADDRESS: 1725 North Main Street
MAILING ADDRESS: 1725 North Main Street
CITY AND ZIP CODE: Santa Monica, Ca 90401
BRANCH NAME: West District

PLAINTIFF/PETITIONER: Virginia E.

DEFENDANT/RESPONDENT: Salvador E.

DECLARATION **APPLICATION FOR SUBPENA DUCES TECUM**	CASE NUMBER:

The undersigned hereby applies for a subpena duces tecum and declares:

1. Trial of this matter has been set for *(date)*: November 14, 1991   In Dept. No.: E   of the above-entitled court

2. *(Name)*: Custodian of the Records of B.F. Plumbing & Heating Co., Inc.
has in his or her possession or under his or her control the following *(specify exact documents, matters, and things to be produced)*
Name of Employee: Salvador E.   Social Security Number: 123-45-6789

   1. Payroll records for the Respondent, Salvador E. for the calendar year 1991, including gross wages, deductions, overtime, bonuses.
   2. Employment records from the date of hire.
   3. Records showing benefits available to dependents of Respondent including health, dental, optometric.

3. The above are material to the issues in the case as follows *(set forth facts fully detailing materiality)*:
I am seeking child support and medical coverage for our minor children. This information is required in order to determine support and what insurance is available to the children.

4. Good cause exists for the production of the above documents, matters, and things as follows:
Respondent will not voluntarily supply the requested information. These items requested are in the possession and control of the Custodian of Records, and there is no other way to obtain the needed information.

I declare under penalty of perjury under the laws of the State of California that the foregoing is true and correct.

Date: October 15, 1991

.................Virginia E................   ▶ *Virginia E.*
(TYPE OR PRINT NAME)   (SIGNATURE OF DECLARANT)

Adapted from
Form Approved by the
Judicial Council of California
MC-030 [New January 1, 1967]

DECLARATION
APPLICATION FOR SUBPENA DUCES TECUM

Figure C-2: Civil Subpoena

ATTORNEY OR PARTY WITHOUT ATTORNEY (Name and Address):

Virginia E.
12345 South Street
City, State, Zip

TELEPHONE NO.: (000) 000-00000

FOR COURT USE ONLY

ATTORNEY FOR (Name): Virginia E., In Pro Per

NAME OF COURT: Los Angeles County Superior Court
STREET ADDRESS: 1725 North Main Street
MAILING ADDRESS: 1725 North Main Street
CITY AND ZIP CODE: Santa Monica, Ca 90401
BRANCH NAME: West District

PLAINTIFF/PETITIONER: Virginia E.

DEFENDANT/RESPONDENT: Salvador E.

CIVIL SUBPENA

[X] Duces Tecum

CASE NUMBER:

THE PEOPLE OF THE STATE OF CALIFORNIA, TO (NAME):
B.F. Plumbing & Heating Co., Inc.,
12345 Venice Boulevard, Los Angeles, CA 90066
(310) 000-0000

1. **YOU ARE ORDERED TO APPEAR AS A WITNESS** in this action at the date, time, and place shown in the box below UNLESS you make a special agreement with the person named in item 3:

   a. Date: November 14, 1991   Time: 9:00 a.m.   [X] Dept.:"E"   [ ] Div.:   [ ] Room:
   b. Address: 1725 North Main Street
   Santa Monica, California 90401

2. AND YOU ARE
   a. [X] ordered to appear in person.
   b. [X] not required to appear in person if you produce the records described in the accompanying affidavit and a completed declaration of custodian of records in compliance with Evidence Code sections 1560, 1561, 1562, and 1271. (1) Place a copy of the records in an envelope (or other wrapper). Enclose your original declaration with the records. Seal them. (2) Attach a copy of this subpena to the envelope or write on the envelope the case name and number, your name and date, time and place from item 1 (the box above). (3) Place this first envelope in an outer envelope, seal it, and mail It to the clerk of the court at the address in item 1. (4) Mail a copy of your declaration to the attorney or party shown at the top of this form.
   c. [ ] ordered to appear in person and to produce the records described in the accompanying affidavit. The **personal attendance** of the custodian or other qualified witness and the production of the original records **is required** by this subpena. The procedure authorized by subdivision (b) of section 1560, and sections 1561 and 1562, of the Evidence Code will not be deemed sufficient compliance with this subpena.

3. IF YOU HAVE ANY QUESTIONS ABOUT THE TIME OR DATE FOR YOU TO APPEAR, OR IF YOU WANT TO BE CERTAIN THAT YOUR PRESENCE IS REQUIRED, CONTACT THE FOLLOWING PERSON BEFORE THE DATE ON WHICH YOU ARE TO APPEAR:
   a. Name: Virginia E.   b. Telephone number: (000) 000-0000

4. **Witness Fees:** You are entitled to witness fees and mileage actually traveled both ways, as provided by law, if you request them at the time of service. You may request them before your scheduled appearance from the person named in item 3.

   DISOBEDIENCE OF THIS SUBPENA MAY BE PUNISHED AS CONTEMPT BY THIS COURT. YOU WILL ALSO BE LIABLE FOR THE SUM OF FIVE HUNDRED DOLLARS AND ALL DAMAGES RESULTING FROM YOUR FAILURE TO OBEY.

Date Issued: October 15, 1991
Clerk of the Court, Deputy _____

▶ _____
(SIGNATURE OF PERSON ISSUING SUBPENA)

(TYPE OR PRINT NAME)

_____
(TITLE)

(See reverse for proof of service)

Form Adopted by Rule 982
Judicial Council of California
982(a)(15) [Rev. January 1, 1991]

CIVIL SUBPENA

Code of Civil Procedure, 1985, 1986, 1987

Figure C-3: Notice to Respondent

Your Name: **Virginia E.**
Address: **12345 South Street**
City, State, Zip: **City, State, Zip**
Telephone: **(123) 456-7890**
For Petitioner In Pro Per

SUPERIOR COURT FOR THE STATE OF CALIFORNIA
FOR THE COUNTY OF **Los Angeles**

In re matter of	) Case Number _____
Petitioner: **Virginia E.**	) NOTICE PURSUANT TO
and	) CCP SECTION 1985.3
Respondent: **Salvador E.**	)

TO THE RESPONDENT, **Salvador E.**

NOTICE IS HEREBY GIVEN THAT:

1. Records pertaining to you are being sought from the persons and/or entities named in the attached subpoena and application attached hereto as Exhibit A, and made a part hereof.

2. If you object to any of said persons and/or entities furnishing such records as provided in said supoena duces tecum, you must file your objection with the above-entitled Court before the date specified for production on the subpoena.

3. You or your attorney may contact me to determine whether I will agree in writing to cancel or limit said subpoena. If I will not agree, and if you do not have an attorney, you should consult an attorney to advise you about your right of privacy, if any, as to said records.

Dated: **10/15/91**

Virginia E.

Figure C-4: Proof of Service

PLAINTIFF/PETITIONER: Virginia E.	CASE NUMBER:
DEFENDANT/RESPONDENT: Salvador E.	

PROOF OF SERVICE OF CIVIL SUBPENA

1. I served this ☐ Subpena ☒ Subpena Duces Tecum and supporting affidavit by personally delivering a copy to the person served as follows:

   a. Person served (name): Custodian of Records of B.F.Plumbing & Heating Co., Inc.

   b. Address where served: 12345 Venice Boulevard
   Los Angeles, CA 90066

   c. Date of delivery: October 16, 1991

   d. Time of delivery: 9:00 a.m.

   e. Witness fees (check one):
   (1) ☐ were offered or demanded
   and paid. Amount: ....$_____
   (2) ☐ were not demanded or paid.

   f. Fee for service: ....$_____

2. I received this subpena for service on (date):

3. Person serving:
   a. ☐ Not a registered California process server.
   b. ☐ California sheriff, marshal, or constable.
   c. ☐ Registered California process server.
   d. ☐ Employee or independent contractor of a registered California process server.
   e. ☐ Exempt from registration under Bus. & Prof. Code section 22350(b).
   f. ☐ Registered professional photocopier.
   g. ☐ Exempt from registration under Bus. & Prof. Code section 22451.
   h. Name, address, and telephone number and, if applicable, county of registration and number:

I declare under penalty of perjury under the laws of the State of California that the foregoing is true and correct.	**(For California sheriff, marshal, or constable use only)** **I certify** that the foregoing is true and correct.
Date:	Date:
▶ _____	▶ _____
(SIGNATURE)	(SIGNATURE)

982(a)(15) [Rev. January 1, 1991]	PROOF OF SERVICE CIVIL SUBPENA	Page two CEB

Figure C-5: Petitioner's Declaration Re Compliance

Your Name: ___**Virginia E.**___

Address: ___**12345 South Street**___

City, State, Zip: ___**City, State, Zip**___

Telephone: ___**(123) 456-7890**___

For Petitioner In Pro Per

SUPERIOR COURT FOR THE STATE OF CALIFORNIA

FOR THE COUNTY OF ___**Los Angeles**___

In re matter of	)	Case Number _____
Petitioner: ___**Virginia E.**___	)))	PETITIONER'S DECLARATION RE COMPLIANCE WITH CCP SECTION 1985.3
and	)))	
Respondent: ___**Salvador E.**___	)))	

I, ___**Virginia E.**___, am the Petitioner in the above entitled action, and I submit this Declaration to certify that I have complied with California Code of Civil Procedure, Section 1985.3 by service of a copy of the attached subpoena to Respondent in accord with the proof of service attached hereto and incorporated herein at this reference.

I declare under penalty of perjury that the foregoing is true and correct.

Executed this ____ day of _____, 199__,

at _____, California.

_____

Figure C-6: Employer's Declaration Re Compliance

Your Name: __B.F. Plumbing & Heating Co. Inc.__
Address: ____12345 Venice Boulevard____
City, State, Zip: __Los Angeles, CA 90066__
Telephone: ___(310) 000-0000_____
For Petitioner In Pro Per

SUPERIOR COURT FOR THE STATE OF CALIFORNIA
FOR THE COUNTY OF __Los Angeles__

In re matter of	) Case Number _____
	)
Petitioner: ___Virginia E.____	) EMPLOYER'S
	) DECLARATION RE COMPLIANCE
and	) WITH EVIDENCE CODE
	) SECTIONS 1560, 1561 AND 1271
Respondent: __Salvador E.___	)
	)
_____	)

I, _____, declare:

1. I am the duly authorized Custodian of Records of

_____

which is located at _____

_____,

telephone _____, hereinafter referred to as "deponent," and have the authority to certify the records produced pursuant to this Subpoena.

2. The attached copies are true and correct copies of all the records described in the Subpoena Duces Tecum, and are made a part hereof.

3. I am making this declaration to verify that these records and all records produced by deponent are trustworthy pursuant to Evidence Code Sections 1560, 1561, and 1271 for the following reasons. These records were made in the regular course of business, at or near the time of the acts, conditions or events noted therein, by the persons who were competent to so complete same. The sources of information and method and time of preparation are such as to indicate the trustworthiness of this information. I declare under penalty of perjury that the foregoing is true and correct.

Executed this ____day of _____, 199__,
at _____, California.

_____

BLANK FORMS

Blank forms included

• Indicates forms that are used in every case. Others are used only if required by the circumstances of your particular case.

- • Application and Declaration for Order
- • Order to Show Cause and Temporary Restraining Order
- • Restraining Order After Hearing
- • Proof of Service

  Additional Page

  Declaration Under UCCJA

  Income and Expense forms set:

    Income and Expense Declaration

    Income Information

    Expense Information

    Child Support Information

  Wage and Earnings Assignment Order

- • Declaration

  Application for Reissuance of Order to Show Cause

  Domestic Violence Order Attachment (Order Attachment 1)

  Order Attachment 2

  Order Attachment 3

  Declaration Application for Subpoena Duces Tecum

  Civil Subpoena / Proof of Service

  Notice to Respondent

  Petitioner's Declaration

  Employer's Declaration

- • Responsive Declaration *(a blank is served on Respondent)*

Judicial Council forms are Martin Dean's Essential Forms, courtesy of Martin Dean, Cavalcade of Law Office Technology, San Francisco.

ATTORNEY OR PARTY WITHOUT ATTORNEY *(Name and Address)*:	TELEPHONE NO.:	FOR COURT USE ONLY

ATTORNEY FOR *(Name)* :

SUPERIOR COURT OF CALIFORNIA, COUNTY OF

STREET ADDRESS:

MAILING ADDRESS:

CITY AND ZIP CODE:

BRANCH NAME:

PERSON TO BE PROTECTED:

PERSON TO BE RESTRAINED:

☐ PETITIONER/PLAINTIFF
☐ RESPONDENT/DEFENDANT
☐ PETITIONER/PLAINTIFF
☐ RESPONDENT/DEFENDANT

APPLICATION AND DECLARATION FOR ORDER
(Domestic Violence Prevention Act)
☐ DECLARATION UNDER UNIFORM CUSTODY OF MINORS ACT

CASE NUMBER:

(THIS IS NOT AN ORDER)

Read the instructions for Obtaining Orders Prohibiting Domestic Violence before completing this form. This form must be completed and filed with Order to Show Cause and Temporary Restraining Order (Form 1296.10).

1. PERSON TO BE PROTECTED *(name)* :
   (Insert in Item 1 names of all persons to be protected by this order.)

2. PERSON TO BE RESTRAINED *(name)* :

Sex: ☐ M ☐ F Ht.: _____ Wt.: _____ Hair Color: _____ Eye Color: _____ Race: _____ Age: _____ Date of birth: _____

3. I am applying for a protective order and *(check at least one)* :
   a. ☐ The person restrained and I *(check at least one)* :
      (1) ☐ are married and a dissolution, legal separation, or nullity proceeding
         (a) ☐ is pending *(if known, specify case no.)* : _____
         (b) ☐ is not pending.
      (2) ☐ were formerly married to each other.
      (3) ☐ are related to each other by blood, marriage, or adoption.
      (4) ☐ live together or cohabit.
      (5) ☐ formerly lived together or cohabited.
      (6) ☐ have had a dating or engagement relationship.
      (7) ☐ are parents together of a child and the male parent is the presumed father under Family Code section 6200 et seq.
      (8) ☐ have a minor child in common and an action has been filed under the Uniform Parentage Act.
   b. ☐ I am a child ☐ who is a juvenile court dependent *(if known, specify case no.)* : _____
      (1) ☐ of a party.
      (2) ☐ who is the subject of an action under the Uniform Parentage Act and my male parent is my presumed father.

Describe in detail the most recent incidents of abuse. State what happened, the dates, who did what to whom, and describe any injuries. Also describe any history of abuse. If more space is needed, attach additional pages and check this box: ☐

(Continued on reverse)

Page one of four

Form Adopted by Rule 1296
Judicial Council of California
1296 [Rev. January 1, 1994]
Martin Dean's Essential Forms ™

APPLICATION AND DECLARATION
(Domestic Violence Prevention)

Family Code, § 6200

PERSON TO BE PROTECTED (Name):	CASE NUMBER:
PERSON TO BE RESTRAINED (Name):	

(THIS IS NOT AN ORDER)

4. The person restrained has intentionally or recklessly (check at least one):
   a. ☐ caused or attempted bodily injury to me or another.
   b. ☐ caused or attempted sexual assault on me or another.
   c. ☐ made me afraid of physical or emotional harm.
   d. ☐ made a family or household member (names):   afraid of physical or emotional harm.

5. The person restrained and I (you must check a or b):
   a. ☐ have no minor children.
   b. ☐ have children ☐ who are juvenile court dependents (if known, specify case no's.): _____

             Child's name   Birthdate

   c. **If you are seeking an order regarding custody or visitation of minor children, complete the following:**
   (1) Each child is now living with
       ☐ me   ☐ person to be restrained at (address optional):
   (2) ☐ Each child has lived only with me or the person to be restrained or both during the last five years.
   (3) ☐ I have not participated in any litigation or proceeding in any state concerning custody of this child.
   (4) ☐ I have no information of any pending custody proceeding or any person not a party to this proceeding who has physical custody or visitation rights concerning this minor child.
   (5) If you have **not** checked a box in each of items (1) through (4), you must attach a completed Declaration Under Uniform Custody of Minors Act form (Form no. MC-150) and check this box: ☐ and the box at the top of the first page.

REQUEST THE COURT TO MAKE THE ORDERS INDICATED BY THE CHECK MARKS IN THE BOXES BELOW.

6. ☐ **RESTRAINING ORDERS**   ☐ **To be ordered now and effective until the hearing.**
   Restrained person must not contact, molest, attack, strike, threaten, sexually assault, batter, telephone or otherwise disturb my peace ☐ and that of the following family or household members (names):

7. ☐ **RESIDENCE EXCLUSION AND RELATED ORDERS**   ☐ **To be ordered now and effective until the hearing.**
   Restrained person must immediately move from and must not return to (address):

   and may take only personal clothing and effects.
   I have a legal right to live at the address above because (specify facts and attach any document that supports your claim):

8. ☐ **STAY-AWAY ORDERS**   ☐ **To be ordered now and effective until the hearing.**
   Restrained person, who resides at (state address if known):
   and works at (state address if known):
   must stay at least (specify):   yards away from the following persons and places (the addresses of the places are optional and you do not have to reveal them):
   a. Myself
       ☐ and the following family or household members (names):

   b. ☐ My residence (address optional):

   c. ☐ My place of work (address optional):

   d. ☐ The children's school or place of child care (address optional):

   e. ☐ Other (specify):
       (address optional):

(Continued on next page)

1296 [Rev. January 1, 1994]
Martin Dean's Essential Forms ™

APPLICATION AND DECLARATION
(Domestic Violence Prevention)

Family Code, § 6200

PERSON TO BE PROTECTED *(Name)* :	CASE NUMBER:
PERSON TO BE RESTRAINED *(Name)* :	

(THIS IS NOT AN ORDER)

▢. ☐ CHILD CUSTODY AND VISITATION ☐ **To be ordered now and effective until the hearing.**

    a. ☐ **Custody** *(see Instructions for Obtaining Orders Prohibiting Domestic Violence for an explanation of physical, legal, sole, and joint custody)*

        I request the custody orders shown in the following columns:

List the child's name below	List the name of the parent who should get **sole physical custody** of the child below *(if you want physical custody to be joint, write the word "joint")*	List the name of the parent who should get **sole legal custody of** the child below *(if you want legal custody to be joint, write the word "joint")*

    b. ☐ **Visitation**

        Restrained person should have the right to visit the children as follows:

        (1) ☐ None.

        (2) ☐ Supervised visitation.

        (3) ☐ Visitation with the following restrictions *(specify)* :

    c. I need this custody and visitation order because of the following facts *(specify)* :

[If you request an order for child support, attorney fees, or costs, attach a completed Income and Expense Declaration (Form no. 1285.50).]

0. ☐ CHILD SUPPORT

    a. ☐ I am receiving public assistance.

    b. ☐ Restrained person should be ordered to pay support as specified, commencing on *(date)* :

Child's name	Birthdate	Monthly Amount

    c. ☐ I request that a wage assignment be issued.

1. ☐ PROPERTY CONTROL ☐ **To be ordered now and effective until the hearing.**

    a. I request that I be given the exclusive temporary use, possession, and control of the following property we own or are buying *(specify)* :

    b. The order is necessary because *(specify)* :

(Continued on reverse)   **Page three of four**

1296 [Rev. January 1, 1994]
Martin Dean's Essential Forms ™

APPLICATION AND DECLARATION
(Domestic Violence Prevention)

PERSON TO BE PROTECTED (Name) :	CASE NUMBER:
PERSON TO BE RESTRAINED (Name) :	

(THIS IS NOT AN ORDER)

12. ☐ **ATTORNEY FEES AND COSTS**
Restrained person should be ordered to pay attorney fees and costs as follows:

13. ☐ **RESTITUTION**
I request that restrained person should be ordered to pay the following lost earnings and other actual expenses or cost of services caused directly by the violence complained of:

<u>Type of loss</u>   <u>Pay to</u>   <u>Amount of claim</u>
$

14. ☐ **COUNSELING**
   a. ☐ I request that restrained person be ordered to participate in batterer's treatment counseling.
   b. ☐ I will continue to live with restrained person and I request that we both be ordered to participate in counseling at separate times and places ☐ and that restrained person, who is able to do so, be ordered to pay the costs of the counseling.

15. ☐ **OTHER ORDERS** (specify other orders you request to help carry out the orders previously requested) :

16. I request that copies of orders be given to the following law enforcement agencies:
   <u>Law Enforcement Agency</u>   <u>Address</u>

17. ☐ **I request that time for service of the Order to Show Cause and accompanying papers be shortened so that they may be served no less than** (specify number): **days before the time set for the hearing.** I need to have the order shortening time because of the facts contained in this application. (Add additional facts if necessary) :

18. ☐ I have been involved in other actions with the restrained person in which restraining orders were issued. (If known, please specify case numbers or, if available, attach copies of orders) : _____

19. ☐ I request a court order waiving the fees payable to a law enforcement agency for serving restraining orders on the restrained person. A completed Application for Waiver of Court Fees and Costs is filed with this application.

I declare under penalty of perjury under the laws of the State of California that the foregoing is true and correct.

Date:

▶

....   _____
(TYPE OR PRINT NAME)   (SIGNATURE OF PERSON TO BE PROTECTED)

Page four of four

296 [Rev. January 1, 1994]
Martin Dean's Essential Forms ™

APPLICATION AND DECLARATION
(Domestic Violence Prevention)

ATTORNEY OR PARTY WITHOUT ATTORNEY *(Name and Address)*:

TELEPHONE NO.:

FOR COURT USE ONLY

ATTORNEY FOR *(Name)*:

SUPERIOR COURT OF CALIFORNIA, COUNTY OF

STREET ADDRESS:

MAILING ADDRESS:

CITY AND ZIP CODE:

BRANCH NAME:

PERSON TO BE PROTECTED:

PERSON TO BE RESTRAINED:

☐ PETITIONER/PLAINTIFF
☐ RESPONDENT/DEFENDANT
☐ PETITIONER/PLAINTIFF
☐ RESPONDENT/DEFENDANT

ORDER TO SHOW CAUSE AND TEMPORARY RESTRAINING ORDER (CLETS)
(Domestic Violence Prevention Act)

CASE NUMBER:

PERSON TO BE PROTECTED *(name)*:
(Insert in item 1 names of all persons to be protected by this order.)

PERSON TO BE RESTRAINED *(name)*:

Sex: ☐ M ☐ F Ht.: _____ Wt.: _____ Hair Color: _____ Eye Color: _____ Race: _____ Age: _____ Date of birth: _____

To Person to be Restrained:
You have the right to attend the court hearing and oppose the application, with or without an attorney at the date, time, and place shown in the box below to give any legal reason why the orders sought in the attached application should not be granted. If you do not attend the court hearing, the court may grant the requested orders, which may last up to 3 years without further notice to you.

Date: Time: Dept.: Room:

TEMPORARY RESTRAINING ORDER

This order shall expire at the date and time of the hearing shown in the box above unless extended by the court.

☐ UNTIL THE TIME OF HEARING, IT IS ORDERED
3. ☐ Person to be restrained shall not contact, molest, attack, strike, threaten, sexually assault, batter, telephone or disturb the peace of the person to be protected ☐ and the following family and household members *(names)*:

4. ☐ Person to be restrained must immediately move from *(address)*:
and take only personal clothing and effects needed until the hearing.
5. ☐ Person to be restrained is ordered to stay at least *(specify)*: yards away from the person to be protected and the following persons and places *(the addresses of these places are optional and you do not have to reveal them)*:
  a. ☐ Protected person's family and household members *(name)*:
  b. ☐ Protected person's residence *(address optional)*:
  c. ☐ Protected person's place of work *(address optional)*:
  d. ☐ The children's school or place of child care *(address optional)*:
  e. ☐ Other *(specify)*:
    (address optional):

Violation of this temporary restraining order is a misdemeanor, punishable by a $1,000 fine, one year in jail, or both or may be punishable as a felony. This order shall be enforced by all law enforcement officers in the State of California. Penal Code section 12021g prohibits any person subject to a restraining order from purchasing or attempting to purchase or otherwise obtain a firearm. Such conduct is subject to a $1,000 fine and imprisonment.

(Temporary Restraining Order continued on reverse)

ORDER TO SHOW CAUSE AND
TEMPORARY RESTRAINING ORDER (CLETS)
(Domestic Violence Prevention)

Family Code § 6200 et seq.

6. ☐ Care, custody, and control of the following minor children are temporarily awarded to protected person:

Child's Name

7. ☐ Exclusive temporary use, possession, and control of the following property are given to protected person:

8. ☐ OTHER ORDERS *(specify)* :

9. ☐ By the close of business on the date of this order a copy of this order and any proof of service shall be given to the law en-forcement agencies listed below as follows:
   a. ☐ Protected person shall deliver.
   b. ☐ Protected person's attorney shall deliver.
   c. ☐ The clerk of the court shall mail.

   Law enforcement agency   Address

10. ☐ Fees for service of this order by law enforcement agencies are waived.
11. ☐ Application for an order shortening time is granted and the following documents shall be personally served on the defendant no less than *(specify number)* :   days before the time set for hearing:
   a. Order to Show Cause and Temporary Restraining Order (Domestic Violence Prevention)
   b. Application and Declaration (Domestic Violence Prevention)
   c. Blank Responsive Declaration (Domestic Violence Prevention)
   d. ☐ Income and Expense Declaration
   e. ☐ Declaration under Uniform Custody of Minors Act.
   f. ☐ Other *(specify)* :

▶

Date: _____

JUDGE OF THE SUPERIOR COURT

This order is effective when made. It is enforceable anywhere in California by any law enforcement agency that has received the order, is shown a copy of it, or has verified its existence on the California Law Enforcement Telecommunications System (CLETS).
If proof of service on the restrained person has not been received, and the restrained person was not present at the court hearing, the law enforcement agency shall advise the restrained person of the terms of the order and then shall enforce it.

(SEAL)

CLERK'S CERTIFICATE
I certify that the foregoing Order to Show Cause and Temporary Restraining Order (CLETS) is a true and correct copy of the original on file in the court.

Date: _____   Clerk, by _____ , Deputy

96.10 [Rev. January 1, 1994]
artin Dean's Essential Forms ™

**ORDER TO SHOW CAUSE AND
TEMPORARY RESTRAINING ORDER (CLETS)**
(Domestic Violence Prevention)

Page two

ATTORNEY OR PARTY WITHOUT ATTORNEY *(Name and Address):*	TELEPHONE NO.:	FOR COURT USE ONLY

ATTORNEY FOR *(Name)*:

SUPERIOR COURT OF CALIFORNIA, COUNTY OF

STREET ADDRESS:

MAILING ADDRESS:

CITY AND ZIP CODE:

BRANCH NAME:

PERSON TO BE PROTECTED:

PERSON TO BE RESTRAINED:

- ☐ PETITIONER/PLAINTIFF
- ☐ RESPONDENT/DEFENDANT
- ☐ PETITIONER/PLAINTIFF
- ☐ RESPONDENT/DEFENDANT

RESTRAINING ORDER AFTER HEARING (CLETS) **(Domestic Violence Prevention)**	CASE NUMBER:

This form may be used in conjunction with the Findings and Order After Hearing form (rule 1296.31) if the court makes additional orders.

. This proceeding was heard

on *(date)* :   at *(time)* :   in Dept.:   Room:

by judge *(name)* :   ☐ Temporary Judge

a. ☐ Petitioner/plaintiff and respondent/defendant were personally present at the court hearing. No additional proof of service of these restraining orders is required.

b. ☐ Petitioner/plaintiff was personally present and proof of service of the Order to Show Cause was provided.

THE COURT FINDS

a. The restrained person is *(name)* :

Sex: ☐ M ☐ F   Ht.: _____   Wt.: _____   Hair Color: _____   Eye Color: _____   Race: _____   Age: _____   Date of birth: _____

b. The protected person is *(name)* :

c. The protected family and household members are *(names)* :

THE COURT ORDERS

THIS ORDER, EXCEPT FOR ANY AWARD OF CHILD CUSTODY OR VISITATION, SHALL EXPIRE AT MIDNIGHT ON *(date)* :

. The restrained person

a. **shall not** contact, molest, attack, strike, threaten, sexually assault, batter, telephone, or disturb the peace of the protected person ☐ and family or household members.

b. ☐ **shall** stay at least _____ yards away from the protected persons and

   (1) ☐ protected person's residence

   (2) ☐ protected person's workplace

   (3) ☐ protected person's children's school or child care

   (4) ☐ other *(specify)* :

     ☐ except as provided in item 5b (visitation).

c. ☐ **shall** immediately move from *(address)* :
   and take only personal clothing and effects.

Taking or concealing a child in violation of this order may be a felony and punishable by confinement in state prison, a fine, or both. Any person subject to a restraining order is prohibited from obtaining or purchasing or attempting to purchase a firearm by Penal Code section 12021. Such conduct may be a felony and punishable by a $1,000 fine and imprisonment. Other violations of this order may also be felonies punishable by fines or imprisonment, or both.

(Continued on reverse)

Form Adopted by Rule 1296.29
Judicial Council of California
296.29 [Rev. January 1, 1994]
Martin Dean's Essential Forms ™

RESTRAINING ORDER AFTER HEARING (CLETS)
(Domestic Violence Prevention)

Family Code, § 6200 et seq.

PERSON TO BE PROTECTED *(Name)*:

PERSON TO BE RESTRAINED *(Name)*:

CASE NUMBER:

. a. ☐ Custody of the minor children

Child's Name	Physical Custody is awarded to *(specify name of parent or "joint")*	Legal Custody is awarded to *(specify name of parent or "joint")*
(1)		
(2)		
(3)		
(4)		
(5)		
(6)		

b. Parent without physical custody *(name)* :
   (1) ☐ shall **not** have visitation
   (2) ☐ shall have visitation as follows *(specify times and conditions, if any)* :

6. ☐ Fees for service of this order by law enforcement agencies are waived.

7. By the close of judicial business on the date of this order, a copy of this order shall be delivered by the protected person to the law enforcement agency having jurisdiction over the residence of the protected person, who shall provide information to assist in identifying the restrained person. Proof of service of this order on the restrained person shall also be provided to the law enforcement agency unless the order shows the restrained person was present in court. The law enforcement agency having jurisdiction over the plaintiff's residence is *(name and address of agency)* :

8. ☐ A copy of this order shall be given to the additional law enforcement agencies listed below as follows:
   (1) ☐ Person to be protected shall deliver.   (2) ☐ Person to be protected's attorney shall deliver.
   (3) ☐ The clerk of the court shall mail.
         Law enforcement agency   Address

. Other *(specify)* :

Date: _____

▶ _____
JUDGE OF THE SUPERIOR COURT

This order is effective when made. It is enforceable anywhere in California by any law enforcement agency that has received the order, is shown a copy of it, or has verified its existence on California Law Enforcement Telecommunications System (CLETS). If proof of service on the restrained person has not been received, and the restrained person was not present at the court hearing, the law enforcement agency shall advise the restrained person of the terms of the order and shall then enforce it.

(SEAL)

CLERK'S CERTIFICATE
I certify that the foregoing Restraining Order After Hearing (CLETS) is a true and correct copy of the original on file in the court.

Date : _____   Clerk, by _____ , Deputy

RESTRAINING ORDER AFTER HEARING (CLETS)
(Domestic Violence Prevention)

ATTORNEY OR PARTY WITHOUT ATTORNEY *(Name and Address)*:	TELEPHONE NO.:	FOR COURT USE ONLY
ATTORNEY FOR *(Name)* :		

SUPERIOR COURT OF CALIFORNIA, COUNTY OF
STREET ADDRESS:

MAILING ADDRESS:

CITY AND ZIP CODE:

BRANCH NAME:

PLAINTIFF:

DEFENDANT:

PROOF OF SERVICE	CASE NUMBER:

PERSONAL SERVICE

Instruction: *After having the other party served with a copy of the document identified in item 1, attach a completed Proof of Service to the original or a true copy of the original and give it to the clerk for filing. Neither the plaintiff nor the defendant can serve these papers.*

. I served a copy of the following documents *(check the box before the title of each document you served)* :

DOMESTIC VIOLENCE

a. ☐ Order to Show Cause and Temporary Restraining Order (Domestic Violence Prevention - Uniform Parentage)

b. ☐ Application and Declaration (Domestic Violence Prevention - Uniform Parentage)

c. ☐ Blank Responsive Declaration (Domestic Violence Prevention - Uniform Parentage)

d. ☐ Income and Expense Declaration

e. ☐ Declaration under Uniform Custody of Minors Act

f. ☐ Application and Order for Re-issuance of order to Show Cause (Domestic Violence Prevention - Uniform Parentage - Family Law)

g. ☐ Order After Hearing (Family Law - Domestic Violence Prevention - Uniform Parentage)

h. ☐ Other *(specify)* :

HARASSMENT

i. ☐ Order to Show Cause and Temporary Restraining Order

j. ☐ Petition for Injunction Prohibiting Harassment

k. ☐ Blank Response to Petition for Injunction Prohibiting Harassment

l. ☐ Other *(specify)* :

EMANCIPATION

m. ☐ Petition for Declaration of Emancipation;

n. ☐ Petition for Recission of Declaration of Emancipation;

PARENTAGE

o. ☐ Complaint to Establish Parental Relationship (Uniform Parentage Act)

OTHER

p. ☐ *(Specify)* :

. Person served *(name)*:

. By personally delivering copies to the person served, as follows:
(1) Date: (2) Time:
(3) Address:

. At the time of service I was at least 18 years of age and **not a party to this cause.**

. I declare under penalty of perjury under the laws of the State of California that the foregoing is true and correct.
Date:

▶

(TYPE OR PRINT NAME)	(SIGNATURE)

(See reverse for proof of service by mail)

Form Adopted by Rule 1296.40
Judicial Council of California
1296.40 [Rev. January 1, 1985]
Martin Dean's Essential Forms ™

PROOF OF SERVICE

PLAINTIFF *(name)* :	CASE NUMBER:
DEFENDANT *(name)* :	

SERVICE BY MAIL

Most of the documents listed on the reverse must be served by personal delivery. Fill out this side only for those documents that can be served by mail.

Instructions: *After serving the other party by mail with a copy of the document identified in item 1, attach a completed Proof of Service to the original or to a true copy of the original and give it to the clerk for filing. An unsigned copy of the Proof of Service should be attached to and served with the document.*

6. I am over the age of 18 and **not a party to this cause.** I am a resident of or employed in the county where the mailing occurred. My residence or business address is:

7. I served a copy of the following documents *(list documents)* :

by placing a true copy of each document in the United States mail, in a sealed envelope with postage fully prepaid, as follows:

a. Date of deposit:

b. Place of deposit *(city and state)*:

c. Addressed as follows:

I declare under penalty of perjury under the laws of the State of California that the foregoing is true and correct.

Date:

(TYPE OR PRINT NAME)	(SIGNATURE)

SHORT TITLE:

CASE NUMBER:

1

2

3

4

5

6

7

8

9

10

11

12

13

14

15

16

17

18

19

20

21

22

23

24

25

26 *(Required for verified pleading)* The items on this page stated on information and belief are *(specify item numbers, not line numbers):*

27

This page may be used with any Judicial Council form or any other paper filed with the court .

Page_____

Form Approved by the
Judicial Council of California
MC-020 [New January 1, 1987]
Martin Dean's Essential Forms ™

ADDITIONAL PAGE
Attach to Judicial Council Form or Other Court Paper

CRC 201, 501
[E116]

ATTORNEY OR PARTY WITHOUT ATTORNEY *(Name and Address)*:

TELEPHONE NO.:

FOR COURT USE ONLY

ATTORNEY FOR *(Name)*:

SUPERIOR COURT OF CALIFORNIA, COUNTY OF

STREET ADDRESS:

MAILING ADDRESS:

CITY AND ZIP CODE:

BRANCH NAME:

CASE NAME:

**DECLARATION UNDER
UNIFORM CHILD CUSTODY JURISDICTION ACT (UCCJA)**

CASE NUMBER:

I am a party to this proceeding to determine custody of a child.

☐ Declarant's present address is not disclosed. It is confidential under Civil Code 5158. The address of children presently residing with declarant is identified on this declaration as confidential.

(Number): minor children are subject to this proceeding as follows:

(Insert the information requested below. The residence information must be given for the last FIVE years.)

a. Child's name		Place of birth		Date of birth	Sex
Period of residence	Address		Person child lived with *(name and present address)*		Relationship
to present	☐ Confidential				
to					
to					
to					

b. Child's name		Place of birth		Date of birth	Sex
☐ Residence information is the same as given above for child **a.** *(If NOT the same, provide the information below.)*					
Period of residence	Address		Person child lived with *(name and present address)*		Relationship
to present	☐ Confidential				
to					
to					

c. ☐ Additional children are listed on Attachment 3c. *(Provide requested information for additional children on an attachment.)*

(Continued on reverse)

Form Approved by the
Judicial Council of California
MC-150 [Rev. January 1, 1993]
Martin Dean's Essential Forms ™

**DECLARATION UNDER
UNIFORM CHILD CUSTODY JURISDICTION ACT (UCCJA)**

Civil Code, § 5158
Probate Code, §§ 1510(f), 1512

Have you participated as a party or a witness or in some other capacity in another litigation or custody proceeding , in California or elsewhere, concerning custody of a child subject to this proceeding?

☐ No ☐ Yes *(If yes, provide the following information:)*

a. Name of each child:

b. Capacity of declarant: ☐ party ☐ witness ☐ other *(specify)* :

c. Court *(specify name, state, location)* :

d. Court order or judgment *(date)* :

Do you have information about a custody proceeding pending in a California court or any other court concerning a child subject to this proceeding, other than that stated in item 4?

☐ No ☐ Yes *(If yes, provide the following information:)*

a. Name of each child:

b. Nature of proceeding: ☐ dissolution or divorce ☐ guardianship ☐ adoption ☐ other *(specify)*:

c. Court *(specify name, state, location)*:

d. Status of proceeding:

Do you know of any person who is not a party to this proceeding who has physical custody or claims to have custody of or visitation rights with any child subject to this proceeding?

☐ No ☐ Yes *(If yes, provide the following information:)*

a. Name and address of person	b. Name and address of person	c. Name and address of person
☐ Has physical custody ☐ Claims custody rights ☐ Claims visitation rights	☐ Has physical custody ☐ Claims custody rights ☐ Claims visitation rights	☐ Has physical custody ☐ Claims custody rights ☐ Claims visitation rights
Name of each child	Name of each child	Name of each child

I declare under penalty of perjury under the laws of the State of California that the foregoing is true and correct.

Date:

▶

.... _____

(TYPE OR PRINT NAME)   (SIGNATURE OF DECLARANT)

☐ Number of pages attached after this page:

NOTICE TO DECLARANT: You have a continuing duty to inform this court if you obtain any information about a custody proceeding in a California court or any other court concerning a child subject to this proceeding.

ATTORNEY OR PARTY WITHOUT ATTORNEY (Name and Address):	TELEPHONE NO.:	FOR COURT USE ONLY

ATTORNEY FOR (Name):

SUPERIOR COURT OF CALIFORNIA, COUNTY OF

STREET ADDRESS:

MAILING ADDRESS:

CITY AND ZIP CODE:

BRANCH NAME:

PETITIONER/PLAINTIFF:

RESPONDENT/DEFENDANT:

INCOME AND EXPENSE DECLARATION	CASE NUMBER:

Step 1
Attachments to summary

I have completed ☐ Income ☐ Expense ☐ Child Support Information forms.
(If child support is not an issue, do not complete the Child Support Information Form. If your only income is AFDC, do not complete the Income Information Form.)

Step 2
Answer all questions that apply to you

1. Are you receiving or have you applied for or do you intend to apply for welfare or AFDC?
☐ Receiving ☐ Applied for ☐ Intend to apply for ☐ No
2. What is your date of birth (month/day/year)? ...._____
3. What is your occupation? _____
4. Highest year of education completed: _____
5. Are you currently employed? ☐ Yes ☐ No
   a. If yes: (1) Where do you work? *(name and address)* : _____
   _____
          (2) When did you start work there *(month/year)* ? .... _____
   b. If no: (1) When did you last work *(month/year)* ? .... _____
          (2) What were your gross monthly earnings? .... _____
6. What is the total number of minor children you are legally obligated to support? .... _____

Step 3
Monthly Income Information

7. Net monthly disposable income *(from line 16a of Income Information)* : .... $ _____

8. Current net monthly disposable income *(If different from line 7, explain below or on Attachment 8)*: $ _____

Step 4
Expense Information

9. Total monthly expenses from line 2q of Expense Information: .... $. _____
10. Amount of these expenses paid by others: .... $. _____

Step 5 Other party's Income

12. My estimate of the other party's gross monthly income is: .... $ _____

Step 6
Date and sign this form

I declare under penalty of perjury under the laws of the State of California that the foregoing and the attached information forms are true and correct.

Date:

▶ _____

_____   _____
(TYPE OR PRINT NAME)   (SIGNATURE OF DECLARANT)

☐ Petitioner ☐ Respondent

Page one of _____

Form Adopted by Rule 1285.50
Judicial Council of California
1285.50 [Rev. January 1, 1995]
Martin Dean's Essential Forms ™

INCOME AND EXPENSE DECLARATION
(Family Law)

PETITIONER/PLAINTIFF:	CASE NUMBER:
RESPONDENT/DEFENDANT:	
INCOME INFORMATION OF (*name*):	

Total gross salary or wages, including commissions, bonuses, and overtime paid during last 12 months: 1. $ _____

All other money received during last 12 months **except welfare, AFDC,**   *Specify sources below:*
SSI, spousal support from this marriage, or any child support.   _____   2a. $ _____

Include pensions, social security, disability, unemployment, military basic allowance for quarters (BAQ), spousal support from a different marriage, dividends, interest or royalty, trust income, and annuities.   2b. $ _____

Include income from a business and rental properties, and reimbursement of _____   2c. $ _____
job-related expenses.

► *Prepare and attach a schedule showing gross receipts less cash expenses for each business or rental property.* _____   2d. $ _____

Add lines 1 through 2d..3.... $ _____

Divide line 3 by 12 and place result on line 4a.

	Average last 12 months:	Last month:
Gross income	4a. $ _____	4b. $ _____
State income tax..	5a. $ _____	5b. $ _____
Federal income tax...	6a. $ _____	6b. $ _____
Social Security and Hospital Tax ("FICA" and "MEDI") or self-employment tax, or the amount used to secure retirement or disability benefits	7a. $ _____	7b. $ _____
Health insurance for you and any children you are required to support.....	8a. $ _____	8b. $ _____
State disability insurance:...	9a. $ _____	9b. $ _____
Mandatory union dues:...	10a. $ _____	10b. $ _____
Mandatory retirement and pension fund contributions:........................... *Do not include any deduction claimed in item 7.*	11a. $ _____	11b. $ _____
Court-ordered child support, court-ordered spousal support, and voluntarily paid child support in an amount not more than the guideline amount, **actually being paid for a relationship *other* than that involved in this proceeding:**...........................	12a. $ _____	12b. $ _____
Necessary job-related expenses *(attach explanation)*	13a. $ _____	13b. $ _____
Hardship deduction (Line 4d on Child Support Information Form)	14a. $ _____	14b. $ _____
Add lines 5 through 14 ....**Total monthly deductions:**	15a. $ _____	15b. $ _____
Subtract line 15 from line 4 ....**Net monthly disposable income:**	16a. $ _____	16b. $ _____

AFDC, welfare, spousal support from this marriage, and child support from other relationships received each month:..17... $ _____

Cash and checking accounts:...18... $ _____

Savings, credit union, certificates of deposit, and money market accounts:.........................19. $ _____

Stocks, bonds, and other liquid assets:...20. $ _____

All other property, real or personal *(specify below)* :...21. $ _____

► **Attach a copy of your three most recent pay stubs.**   Page _____ of _____

Form Adopted by Rule 1285.50a
Judicial Council of California
1285.50a [Rev. January 1, 1995]
Martin Dean's Essential Forms ™

INCOME INFORMATION
(Family Law)

PETITIONER/PLAINTIFF:	CASE NUMBER:
RESPONDENT/DEFENDANT:	
EXPENSE INFORMATION OF (name):	

		name	age	relationship	gross monthly income
a. List all persons living in your home **whose expenses are included below** and their income: ☐ Continued on Attachment 1a.	1. 2. 3. 4.				
b. List all other persons living in your home and their income: ☐ Continued on Attachment 1b.	1. 2. 3.				

MONTHLY EXPENSES

a. Residence payments

  (1) ☐ Rent or ☐ mortgage........$ _____

  (2) If mortgage, include:

    Average principle ....$ _____

    Average interest ....$ _____

    Impound for real $ _____
      property taxes ....$ _____

    Impound for home-
      owner's insurance ...$ _____

  (3) Real property taxes (if not included in item (2)) ....$ _____

  (4) Homeowner's or renter's insurance (if not included in item (2)) ..... $ _____

  (5) Maintenance.............................$ _____

b. Unreimbursed medical and dental expenses ....$ _____

c. Child care ....$ _____

d. Children's education.........................$ _____

e. Food at home and household supplies $ _____

f. Food eating out....................................$ _____

g. Utilities ....$ _____

h. Telephone ....$ _____

i. Laundry and cleaning ....$ _____

j. Clothing ....$ _____

k. Insurance (life, accident, etc. Do not include auto, home, or health insurance) $ _____

l. Education (specify): ....$ _____

m. Entertainment ....$ _____

n. Transportation and auto expenses (insurance, gas, oil, repair) ....$ _____

o. Installment payments (insert total and itemize below in item 3) ....$ _____

p. Other (amount): ....$ _____

q. TOTAL EXPENSES (a-p) ....$ _____
  (do not include amounts in a (2))

ITEMIZATION OF INSTALLMENT PAYMENTS OR OTHER DEBTS ☐ Continued on Attachment 3.

CREDITOR'S NAME	PAYMENT FOR	MONTHLY PAYMENT	BALANCE	DATE LAST PAYMENT MADE

ATTORNEY FEES

a. I have paid my attorney for fees and costs: $ [_____]   The source of this money was:

b. I owe to date the following fees and costs over the amount paid:

c. My arrangement for attorney fees and costs is:

    I confirm this information and fee arrangement.   ▶

        (SIGNATURE OF ATTORNEY)

....
        (TYPE OR PRINT NAME OF ATTORNEY)

Page _____ **of** _____

Form Adopted by Rule 1285.50b
Judicial Council of California
1285.50b [Rev. January 1, 1995]
Martin Dean's Essential Forms ™

EXPENSE INFORMATION
(Family Law)

PETITIONER/PLAINTIFF:	CASE NUMBER:
RESPONDENT/DEFENDENT:	
CHILD SUPPORT INFORMATION OF *(name)* :	

THIS PAGE MUST BE COMPLETED IF CHILD SUPPORT IS AN ISSUE.

1. Health insurance for my children ☐ is ☐ is not available through my employer.
   a. Monthly cost paid by me or on my behalf for the children *only* is: $ _____
      Do not include the amount paid or payable by your employer.
   b. Name of carrier:
   c. Address of carrier:

   d. Policy or group policy number:

2. Approximate percentage of time each parent has primary physical responsibility for the children:
   Mother   % Father   %

3. ☐ The court is requested to order the following as additional child support:
   a. ☐ Child care costs related to employment or to reasonably necessary education or training for employment skills
      (1) Monthly amount presently paid by mother: $
      (2) Monthly amount presently paid by father: $
   b. ☐ Uninsured health care costs for the children *(for each cost state the purpose for which the cost was incurred and the estimated monthly, yearly, or lump sum amount paid by each parent)* :

   c. ☐ Educational or other special needs of the children *(for each cost state the purpose for which the cost was incurred and the estimated monthly, yearly, or lump sum amount paid by each parent)* :

   d. ☐ Travel expense for visitation
      (1) Monthly amount presently paid by mother: $
      (2) Monthly amount presently paid by father: $

4. ☐ The court is requested to allow the deductions identified below, which are justifiable expenses that have caused an extreme financial hardship.

	Amount paid per month	**How many months will you need to make these payments**
a. ☐ Extraordinary health care expenses *(specify and attach any supporting documents)* :	$_____	_____
b. ☐ Uninsured catastrophic losses *(specify and attach any supporting documents)* :	$_____	_____
c. ☐ Minimum basic living expenses of dependent minor children from other marriages or relationships who live with you *(specify names and ages of these children)* :	$_____	_____
d. Total hardship deductions requested *(add lines a-c)* :	$_____	

Page _____ of _____

Form Adopted by Rule 1285.50c
Judicial Council of California
1285.50c [Rev. January 1, 1995]
Martin Dean's Essential Forms ™

CHILD SUPPORT INFORMATION
(Family Law)

ATTORNEY OR PARTY WITHOUT ATTORNEY (Name and Address):   TELEPHONE NO.:   FOR COURT USE ONLY

ATTORNEY FOR (Name):

SUPERIOR COURT OF CALIFORNIA, COUNTY OF
    STREET ADDRESS:
    MAILING ADDRESS:
    CITY AND ZIP CODE:
    BRANCH NAME:

PETITIONER/PLAINTIFF:

RESPONDENT/DEFENDANT:

CASE NUMBER:

WAGE AND EARNINGS ASSIGNMENT ORDER
☐ **Modification**   ☐ **Child Support**   ☐ **Spousal or Family Support**

THE PAYOR: This is a court order. You must withhold a portion of the earnings of (obligor's name and date of birth):

and pay as directed below. (An explanation of this order is printed on the reverse.)

THE COURT ORDERS YOU TO

Pay part of the earnings of the employee or other person ordered to pay support as follows:

a. ☐ $ _____ per month current **child support.** d. ☐ $ _____ per month **child support arrearages.**
b. ☐ $ _____ per month current **spousal support.** e. ☐ $ _____ per month **spousal support arrearages.**
c. ☐ $ _____ per month current **family support.** f. ☐ $ _____ per month **family support arrearages.**
g. Total deductions per month: $ _____

☐ The payments ordered under items 1a, 1b, and 1c shall be paid to (name, address):

☐ The payments ordered under item 1d, 1e, and 1f shall be paid to (name, address):

The payments ordered under item 1 shall continue until further written notice from payee or the court.

☐ This order modifies an existing order. **The amount you must withhold may have changed.** The existing order continues in effect until this modification is effective.

This order affects all earnings payable beginning as soon as possible but not later than 10 days after you receive it.

Give the obligor a copy of this order within 10 days.

☐ Other (specify):

For the purposes of this order, the arrearages are set as follows:
                          Amount   As of (date)
a. ☐ Child support:
b. ☐ Spousal support:
c. ☐ Family support:

Date: _____   _____
                                  JUDGE OF THE SUPERIOR COURT

(See reverse for information and instructions)

Form Adopted by Rule 1285.70
Judicial Council of California
1285.70 [Rev. January 1, 1995]
Martin Dean's Essential Forms ™

WAGE AND EARNINGS ASSIGNMENT ORDER
(Family Law - Domestic Violence Prevention - Uniform Parentage)

Family Code, § 5208
Code of Civil Procedure, § 706.031
15 U.S.C. § § 1672-1673

INFORMATION ABOUT THE
WAGE AND EARNINGS ASSIGNMENT ORDER

1. DEFINITIONS OF IMPORTANT WORDS IN THIS INFORMATION:

A. **Obligor:** any person ordered by a court to pay child support, spousal support, or family support. Named before item 1 on the reverse.

B. **Obligee:** the person to whom the support is to be paid, including the District Attorney or other government agency in some cases. Named in item 2 on the reverse.

C. **Payor:** the person or entity, including an employer, that pays earnings to an obligor.

D. **Earnings:**

(1) wages, salary, bonuses, vacation pay, retirement pay, and commissions paid by an employer;

(2) payments for services of independent contractors;

(3) dividends, rents, royalties, and residuals;

(4) patent rights, mineral or other natural resource rights;

(5) any payments due as a result of written or oral contracts for services or sales, regardless of their title; and

(6) any other payments or credits that result from an enforceable obligation.

E. **Wage and Earnings Assignment Order:** A court order issued in every court case where one person is ordered to pay for the support of another person. The support may be child, spousal, or family support. This order has top priority over any other orders such as garnishments or earnings withholding orders. Earnings should not be withheld for any other order until the amounts necessary to satisfy this order have been withheld in full.

When this order is for child support, it has top priority over a similar order for spousal support. The front of this form tells which types of support this order is for.

2. INFORMATION FOR ALL PAYORS: Withhold money from the earnings payable to the obligor as soon as possible but not later than 10 days after you receive this order. Send it to the obligee within 10 days of the pay date. You may deduct $1.00 from the obligor's earnings for each periodic payment you make.

When sending the withheld earnings to the payee, state the date that the earnings were withheld. If you are unable to pay the withheld amounts for six months or more because the person named in item 2 on the reverse has not notified you of a change of address, make no further payments under this order and return all undeliverable payments to the obligor. You will be liable for any amount you fail to withhold and can be cited for contempt of court.

You may combine amounts withheld for more than one obligor in a single payment to each obligee, if you identify the portion of that payment that is attributable to each obligor.

If you have more than one order for an obligor, you must allocate among these orders following the multiple wage assignments procedure (Form 1285.70A).

3. *SPECIAL COMPUTATION INSTRUCTIONS FOR PAYORS WHO ARE EMPLOYERS:*

A. State and Federal laws limit the amount of earnings that you should withold and pay as directed by this order. This limitation applies only to earnings described in item 1D(1). The limitation is stated as a specified percentage of the employee's disposable earnings.

Disposable earnings are different from gross pay or take-home pay. Disposable earnings are the earnings left after subtracting the money that state or federal law requires an employer to withhold. Generally these required deductions are (1) federal income tax, (2) social security, (3) state income tax, (4) state disability insurance, and (5) payments to public employees' retirement systems.

After the employee's disposable earnings are known, withhold the amount required by the order, BUT NEVER WITHOLD MORE THAN 50 PERCENT OF THE DISPOSABLE EARNINGS UNLESS THE COURT ORDER SPECIFIED A HIGHER PERCENTAGE. Federal law prohibits withholding more than 65 percent of disposable earnings of an employee in any case.

B. If the employee is paid by a different time period from that specified in the order, prorate the amount ordered to be withheld so part of it is withheld from each of the employee's paychecks.

C. If the employee stops working for you, notify the obligee, not later than the date of the next payment, by first class mail, giving the employee's last known address, and, if you know them, the name and address of any new employer.

D. California law prohibits you from firing, refusing to hire, or taking any disciplinary action against any employee because of a Wage and Earnings Assignment Order. Such action can lead to a $500 civil penalty per employee.

4. INFORMATION FOR ALL OBLIGORS: Family Code section 5270 describes the procedures available for you to ask the court to quash this order. You may file a motion to quash this order but you must act within 10 days after you receive a copy of the order from the payor. See the procedure set forth in Family Code section 5271.

Family Code section 5240 describes the procedure by which an obligor may request the court to terminate the assignment order.

These laws may be found in any law library. Each California county has a law library.

5. *SPECIAL INFORMATION FOR THE OBLIGOR WHO IS AN EMPLOYEE:* Family Code section 5281 requires you to notify the obligee (item 2 on the reverse) if you change your employment. You must provide the name and address of your new employer.

ATTORNEY OR PARTY WITHOUT ATTORNEY (Name and Address):

TELEPHONE NO.:

FOR COURT USE ONLY

ATTORNEY FOR (Name):

NAME OF COURT:

STREET ADDRESS:

MAILING ADDRESS:

CITY AND ZIP CODE:

BRANCH NAME:

PLAINTIFF/PETITIONER:

DEFENDANT/RESPONDENT:

DECLARATION

CASE NUMBER:

I declare under penalty of perjury under the laws of the State of California that the foregoing is true and correct.

Date:

▶

....
(TYPE OR PRINT NAME)

_____
(SIGNATURE OF DECLARANT)

☐ Petitioner/Plaintiff   ☐ Respondent/Defendant   ☐ Attorney

☐ Other(specify):

(See reverse for a form to be used if this declaration will be attached to another court form before filing)

Form Approved by the
Judicial Council of California
MC-030 [New January 1, 1987]
Martin Dean's Essential Forms TM

DECLARATION

ATTORNEY OR PARTY WITHOUT ATTORNEY (Name and Address):

TELEPHONE NO.:

FOR COURT USE ONLY

ATTORNEY FOR (Name):

SUPERIOR COURT OF CALIFORNIA, COUNTY OF
    STREET ADDRESS:

    MAILING ADDRESS:

    CITY AND ZIP CODE:

    BRANCH NAME:

PLAINTIFF:

DEFENDANT:

APPLICATION AND ORDER FOR REISSUANCE OF ORDER TO SHOW CAUSE
(Family Law - Domestic Violence Prevention - Uniform Parentage)

CASE NUMBER:

Plaintiff requests the court to reissue the Order to Show Cause and Temporary Restraining Order originally issued as follows:

a. Order To Show Cause was issued on (date):

b. Order To Show Cause was last set for hearing on (date):

c. Order To Show Cause has been reissued previously (number of times):

Plaintiff requests reissuance of the order because:

a. ☐ Defendant was unable to be served as required before the hearing date.

b. ☐ The hearing was continued because the parties were referred to court mediators, reconciliation court, or family court services.

c. ☐ Other (specify):

I declare under penalty of perjury under the laws of the State of California that the foregoing is true and correct.

Date:

....
            (TYPE OR PRINT NAME)

_____
            (SIGNATURE)

ORDER

IT IS ORDERED that the Order To Show Cause issued as shown in item 1 above is re-issued and reset for hearing in this court as follows:

Date: time: dept.:   rm.:

at the street address of the court shown above.

b. By the close of business on the date of this order a copy of this order and any proof of service shall be given to the law enforcement agencies named in the Order To Show Cause as follows:

    ☐ the plaintiff shall deliver.

    ☐ the plaintiff's attorney shall deliver.

    ☐ the clerk of the court shall mail.

c. A copy of this order shall be attached to documents to be served on the defendant, as directed in the Order To Show Cause, and shall also be served on the defendant.

d. All other orders contained in the Order To Show Cause remain in full force and effect unless modified by this order. **THE ORDER TO SHOW CAUSE AND THIS ORDER EXPIRE ON THE DATE AND TIME OF THE HEARING SHOWN IN THE BOX ABOVE UNLESS EXTENDED BY THIS COURT.**

Date:
_____
        JUDGE OF THE SUPERIOR COURT

CLERK'S CERTIFICATE OF MAILING

I certify that I am not a party to this cause and that a copy of the foregoing was mailed first class, postage prepaid, in a sealed envelope addressed as shown in the Order To Show Cause and that the foregoing was mailed and this certificate was executed at

(place):   , California,

(date):   Clerk, by _____ , Deputy

Form Adopted by Rule 1296.15
Judicial Council of California
1296.15 [Rev. January 1, 1985]
Martin Dean's Essential Forms ™

APPLICATION AND ORDER FOR REISSUANCE
OF ORDER TO SHOW CAUSE
(Family Law - Domestic Violence Prevention - Uniform Parentage)

CCP 527(b)

PLAINTIFF *(Name)*:	CASE NUMBER:
DEFENDANT *(Name)*:	

DOMESTIC VIOLENCE MISCELLANEOUS ORDERS ATTACHMENT
(Attachment to Findings and Order After Hearing (rule 1296.31)
-or-
to Restraining Order After Hearing (CLETS) (rule 1296.29))

1. a. ☐ Plaintiff is given exclusive use, possession, and control of the following property:

   b. ☐ Defendant shall make the following payments coming due while this order is in effect:

Debt	Payable to	Amount of payment	Date payable
		$	

2. ☐ Defendant shall pay the following attorney fees and costs:

	Payable to	Amount of payment	Date payable
		$	

3. ☐ Defendant shall make the following payments as restitutuon:

	Payable to	Amount of payment	Date payable
		$	

4. a. ☐ The following parties shall participate in counseling as the court directs: ☐ Plaintiff   ☐ Defendant
   b. ☐ Defendant shall participate in counseling for batterers.

5. ☐ OTHER ORDERS:

If there are minor children of this relationship, obtain an order for child support.
Use the Child Support Order Attachment (Form 1296.31B) or item 5, other orders, on this form.

Page _____ of _____

Form Adopted by Rule 1296.31E
Judicial Council of California
1296.31E [Rev. January 1, 1995]
Martin Dean's Essential Forms ™

DOMESTIC VIOLENCE MISCELLANEOUS ORDERS ATTACHMENT
(Domestic Violence Prevention - Uniform Parentage Act)

Family Code, § § 6324, 6340-6344

PETITIONER (Name):	CASE NUMBER:
RESPONDENT (Name):	

ATTACHMENT ☐ A ☐ B ☐ ___ to the
☐ Order To Show Cause and Temporary Restraining Order
☐ Restraining Order After Hearing

ORDERS RELATING TO CHILDREN:

☐ Neither party shall remove the minor child(ren) from the State of California without the prior written consent of the other party or an order of the court.

☐ Parties must make and keep at least one appointment in Conciliation Court prior to the OSC hearing.

☐ Police shall serve and enforce all TRO's, including but not limited to, escorting Petitioner to Respondent's residence, retrieving the parties' minor child(ren) from the Respondent, and returning the parties' minor child(ren) to Petitioner.

☐ Respondent shall return to Petitioner their minor child(ren) forthwith.

☐ No visitation pending the OSC hearing.

☐ Respondent may have the following visitation pending the OSC hearing:

☐ The Respondent may not use alcohol or drugs within 72 hours of, or during, visitation.

☐ The Respondent may not drive the child(ren) while under the influence of alcohol or drugs.

☐ Neutral pick-up and drop-off location for any visitation (specify location):

ORDER FOR DWELLING EXCLUSION:

☐ Police shall enforce and serve all temporary restraining orders, including but not limited to, escorting Petitioner to the residence, serving Respondent with the TRO and escorting Respondent away from the residence.

☐ Police shall serve and enforce all TRO's.

Number of orders checked above: ___

Dated: _____   _____

Judge of the Superior Court

PETITIONER *(Name):*	CASE NUMBER:
RESPONDENT *(Name):*	

ATTACHMENT ☐ A ☐ B ☐ ___ to the
☐ Order To Show Cause and Temporary Restraining Order
☐ Restraining Order After Hearing

ORDERS RELATING TO PROPERTY OF MARRIED PARTIES:

☐ The Respondent shall be restrained from transferring, encumbering, hypothecating, concealing, or in any way disposing of any property, real or personal, whether community, quasi-community, or separate, except in the usual course of business or for the necessities of life. Applicant shall be notified at least five business days before any proposed extraordinary expenditures and an accounting of such be made to the court.

☐ Both parties are restrained and enjoined from cashing, borrowing against, canceling, transferring, disposing of, or changing the beneficiaries of any insurance or other coverage including life, health, automobile, and disability held for the benefit of the parties or their minor child(ren).

☐ Neither party shall incur any debts or liabilities for which the other party may be held responsible, other than in the ordinary course of business or for the necessities of life.

OTHER ORDERS:

☐ Police shall serve and enforce all TRO's.

☐ Petitioner shall be allowed access to Respondent's residence to retrieve his/her (and/or child(ren)'s) personal belongings with a police escort and until Petitioner has retrieved all such belongings from Respondent's residence.

☐ If the Respondent is served with the TRO at the residence, he/she shall retrieve his/her personal belongings at that time and shall return to Petitioner all keys and copies of keys to the residence. However, if the Respondent is not served with the TRO at the residence, Respondent shall have access to the residence of the Petitioner only once and only with a police escort to retrieve his/her personal belongings, if any, and to return to Petitioner all keys and copies of keys to the residence. The Respondent may otherwise mail the keys to the Petitioner, or give them to a neutral party to return to the Petitioner.

☐ Respondent shall return to Petitioner forthwith Petitioner's (describe):

Number of orders checked above: ___

Dated: _____

_____
Judge of the Superior Court

ATTORNEY OR PARTY WITHOUT ATTORNEY *(Name and Address)*:	TELEPHONE NO.:	FOR COURT USE ONLY

ATTORNEY FOR *(Name)*:

NAME OF COURT:

STREET ADDRESS:

MAILING ADDRESS:

CITY AND ZIP CODE:

BRANCH NAME:

PLAINTIFF/PETITIONER:

DEFENDANT/RESPONDENT:

DECLARATION APPLICATION FOR SUBPENA DUCES TECUM	CASE NUMBER:

The undersigned hereby applies for a subpena duces tecum and declares:

1. Trial of this matter has been set for *(date)*:   in Dept. No.:   of the above-entitled court

2. *(Name)*:

   has in his or her possession or under his or her control the following *(specify exact documents, matters, and things to be produced)*:

3. The above are material to the issues in the case as follows *(set forth facts fully detailing materiality)*:

4. Good cause exists for the production of the above documents, matters, and things as follows:

   I declare under penalty of perjury under the laws of the State of California that the foregoing is true and correct.

Date:

....   ▶   _____

        (TYPE OR PRINT NAME)   *(SIGNATURE OF DECLARANT)*

Adapted from
Form Approved by the
Judicial Council of California
MC-030 [New January 1, 1987]

ATTORNEY OR PARTY WITHOUT ATTORNEY (Name and Address):   TELEPHONE NO.:   **FOR COURT USE ONLY**

ATTORNEY FOR (Name):

NAME OF COURT:

STREET ADDRESS:

MAILING ADDRESS:

CITY AND ZIP CODE:

BRANCH NAME:

PLAINTIFF/PETITIONER:

DEFENDANT/RESPONDENT:

CIVIL SUBPENA   CASE NUMBER:

☐ **Duces Tecum**

THE PEOPLE OF THE STATE OF CALIFORNIA, TO (NAME):

1. **YOU ARE ORDERED TO APPEAR AS A WITNESS** in this action at the date, time, and place shown in the box below **UNLESS** you **make a special agreement with the person named in item 3:**

    a. Date: Time: ☐ Dept.:   ☐ Div.:   ☐ Room:

    b. Address:

2. AND YOU ARE
   a. ☐ ordered to appear in person.
   b. ☐ not required to appear in person if you produce the records described in the accompanying affidavit and a completed declaration of custodian of records in compliance with Evidence Code sections 1560, 1561, 1562, and 1271. (1) Place a copy of the records in an envelope (or other wrapper). Enclose your original declaration with the records. Seal them. (2) Attach a copy of this subpena to the envelope or write on the envelope the case name and number, your name and date, time, and place from item 1 (the box above). (3) Place this first envelope in an outer envelope, seal it, and mail it to the clerk of the court at the address in item 1. (4) Mail a copy of your declaration to the attorney or party shown at the top of this form.
   c. ☐ ordered to appear in person and to produce the records described in the accompanying affidavit. The **personal attendance** of the custodian or other qualified witness and the production of the original records **is required** by this subpena. The procedure authorized by subdivision (b) of section 1560, and sections 1561 and 1562, of the Evidence Code will not be deemed sufficient compliance with this subpena.

3. **IF YOU HAVE ANY QUESTIONS ABOUT THE TIME OR DATE FOR YOU TO APPEAR, OR IF YOU WANT TO BE CERTAIN THAT YOUR PRESENCE IS REQUIRED, CONTACT THE FOLLOWING PERSON BEFORE THE DATE ON WHICH YOU ARE TO APPEAR:**
   a. Name: b. Telephone number:

4. **Witness Fees:** You are entitled to witness fees and mileage actually traveled both ways, as provided by law, if you request them at the time of service. You may request them before your scheduled appearance from the person named in item 3.

DISOBEDIENCE OF THIS SUBPENA MAY BE PUNISHED AS CONTEMPT BY THIS COURT. YOU WILL ALSO BE LIABLE FOR THE SUM OF FIVE HUNDRED DOLLARS AND ALL DAMAGES RESULTING FROM YOUR FAILURE TO OBEY.

Date issued:

▶

....

(TYPE OR PRINT NAME)   (SIGNATURE OF PERSON ISSUING SUBPENA)

(TITLE)

(See reverse for proof of service)

Form Adopted by Rule 982
Judicial Council of California
982(a)(15) [Rev. January 1, 1991]
Martin Dean's Essential Forms TM

CIVIL SUBPENA

Code of Civil Procedure, §§ 1985, 1986, 1987

PLAINTIFF/PETITIONER:	CASE NUMBER:
DEFENDANT/RESPONDENT:	

PROOF OF SERVICE OF CIVIL SUBPENA

I served this ☐ Subpena ☐ Subpena Duces Tecum and supporting affadavit by personally delivering a copy to the person served as follows:

a. Person served *(name)* :

b. Address where served:

c. Date of delivery:

d. Time of delivery:

e. Witness fees *(check one):*
   (1) ☐ were offered or demanded
       and paid. Amount:......$ _____
   (2) ☐ were not demanded or paid.

f. Fee for service: ....$ _____

I received this subpena for service on *(date)* :

Person serving:
a. ☐ Not a registered California process server.
b. ☐ California sheriff, marshal, or constable.
c. ☐ Registered California process server.
d. ☐ Employee or independent contractor of a registered California process server.
e. ☐ Exempt from registration under Bus. & Prof. Code section 22350(b).
f. ☐ Registered professional photocopier.
g. ☐ Exempt from registration under Bus. & Prof. Code section 22451.
h. Name, address, and telephone number and, if applicable, county of registration and number:

I **declare** under penalty of perjury under the laws of the State of California that the foregoing is true and correct.

Date:

_____
(SIGNATURE)

(For California sheriff, marshal, or constable use only)
I **certify** that the foregoing is true and correct.

Date:

▶

_____
(SIGNATURE)

Your Name: _____

Address: _____

City, State, Zip: _____

Telephone: _____

For Petitioner In Pro Per

SUPERIOR COURT FOR THE STATE OF CALIFORNIA

FOR THE COUNTY OF _____

In re matter of   )   Case Number _____
)
Petitioner: _____   )   NOTICE PURSUANT TO
)   CCP SECTION 1985.3
and   )
)
Respondent: _____   )
)
_____)

TO THE RESPONDENT, _____

NOTICE IS HEREBY GIVEN THAT:

1. Records pertaining to you are being sought from the persons and/or entities named in the attached subpoena and application attached hereto as Exhibit A, and made a part hereof.

2. If you object to any of said persons and/or entities furnishing such records as provided in said supoena duces tecum, you must file your objection with the above-entitled Court before the date specified for production on the subpoena.

3. You or your attorney may contact me to determine whether I will agree in writing to cancel or limit said subpoena. If I will not agree, and if you do not have an attorney, you should consult an attorney to advise you about your right of privacy, if any, as to said records.

Dated: _____

_____

Your Name: _____

Address: _____

City, State, Zip: _____

Telephone: _____

For Petitioner In Pro Per

SUPERIOR COURT FOR THE STATE OF CALIFORNIA

FOR THE COUNTY OF _____

In re matter of   )   Case Number _____
)
Petitioner: _____   )   PETITIONER'S
)   DECLARATION RE
and   )   COMPLIANCE WITH
)   CCP SECTION 1985.3
Respondent: _____   )
)
_____)

      I, _____, am the Petitioner in the above entitled action, and I submit this Declaration to certify that I have complied with California Code of Civil Procedure, Section 1985.3 by service of a copy of the attached subpoena to Respondent in accord with the proof of service attached hereto and incorporated herein at this reference.

      I declare under penalty of perjury that the foregoing is true and correct.

Executed this ____day of _____, 199__,

at _____, California.

_____

Your Name: _____

Address: _____

City, State, Zip: _____

Telephone: _____

For Petitioner In Pro Per

SUPERIOR COURT FOR THE STATE OF CALIFORNIA

FOR THE COUNTY OF _____

In re matter of   )   Case Number _____
)
Petitioner: _____   )   EMPLOYER'S
)   DECLARATION RE COMPLIANCE
and   )   WITH EVIDENCE CODE
)   SECTIONS 1560, 1561 AND 1271
Respondent: _____   )
)
_____   )

I, _____, declare:

1. I am the duly authorized Custodian of Records of

_____

which is located at _____

_____,

telephone _____, hereinafter referred to as "deponent," and
have the authority to certify the records produced pursuant to this Subpoena.

2. The attached copies are true and correct copies of all the records described
in the Subpoena Duces Tecum, and are made a part hereof.

3. I am making this declaration to verify that these records and all records
produced by deponent are trustworthy pursuant to Evidence Code Sections 1560,
1561, and 1271 for the following reasons. These records were made in the regular
course of business, at or near the time of the acts, conditions or events noted therein,
by the persons who were competent to so complete same. The sources of information
and method and time of preparation are such as to indicate the trustworthiness of this
information. I declare under penalty of perjury that the foregoing is true and correct.

Executed this ____day of _____, 199__,

at _____, California.

_____

ATTORNEY OR PARTY WITHOUT ATTORNEY (Name and Address): | TELEPHONE NO.: | FOR COURT USE ONLY

ATTORNEY FOR (Name):

SUPERIOR COURT OF CALIFORNIA, COUNTY OF

STREET ADDRESS:

MAILING ADDRESS:

CITY AND ZIP CODE:

BRANCH NAME:

PERSON TO BE PROTECTED:

PERSON TO BE RESTRAINED:

☐ PETITIONER/PLAINTIFF
☐ RESPONDENT/DEFENDANT
☐ PETITIONER/PLAINTIFF
☐ RESPONDENT/DEFENDANT

RESPONSIVE DECLARATION TO ORDER TO SHOW CAUSE
(Domestic Violence Prevention Act)

| HEARING DATE | TIME | DEPT., ROOM, OR DIVISION | CASE NUMBER: |

This response will be considered by the judge at the court hearing. You must still obey the orders granted pending the hearing.

You may ask the court to make orders you request, including restraining orders. You must appear at the court hearing to give the court evidence about orders you request.

If you do not appear at the court hearing, the court may grant the requested orders, which may last up to 3 years without further notice to you.

espond to the Application and Declaration (Domestic Violence Prevention) as follows:

1. ☐ **RESTRAINING ORDERS**
   I ☐ do ☐ do not consent to the order requested.

2. ☐ **RESIDENCE EXCLUSION AND RELATED ORDERS**
   I ☐ do ☐ do not consent to the order requested.

3. ☐ **STAY-AWAY ORDERS**
   I ☐ do ☐ do not consent to the order requested.

4. ☐ **CHILD CUSTODY**
   a. ☐ I consent to the custody order requested.   b. ☐ I request the following custody order:

5. ☐ **CHILD VISITATION**
   a. ☐ I consent to the visitation order requested.   b. ☐ I request the following visitation order:

6. ☐ **CHILD SUPPORT**
   I ☐ do ☐ do not consent to the order requested.

(Continued on reverse)

Form Adopted by Rule 1296.20
Judicial Council of California
1296.20 [Rev. January 1, 1994]
Martin Dean's Essential Forms ™

RESPONSIVE DECLARATION TO ORDER TO SHOW CAUSE
(Domestic Violence Prevention)

Family Code § 6200 et seq.

7. ☐ **PROPERTY CONTROL**
   I ☐ do ☐ do not   consent to the order requested.

8. ☐ **ATTORNEY FEES**
   I ☐ do ☐ do not   consent to the order requested.

9. ☐ **RESTITUTION**
   I ☐ do ☐ do not   consent to the order requested.

10. ☐ **COUNSELING**
   I ☐ do ☐ do not   consent to the order requested.

11. ☐ **OTHER ORDERS** *(see item 15 of the Application and Declaration)*
   I ☐ do ☐ do not   consent to the order requested.

12. ☐ I request the court to order payment of my
   a. ☐ attorney fees if I win.
   b. ☐ out-of-pocket expenses incurred as the result of an ex parte temporary restraining order issued without sufficient
      supporting facts. The expenses are:

   Item   Amount

13. ☐ I request the following additional orders:

14. ☐ **SUPPORTING INFORMATION**
   ☐ contained in the attached declaration

I declare under penalty of perjury under the laws of the State of California that the foregoing is true and correct.

Date:

▶

....
(TYPE OR PRINT NAME)

_____
(SIGNATURE)